You're NOT Broken
You Need to Harness
Your Inner Power

Christine McDowell

Manor House

You're NOT Broken

Library and Archives Canada Cataloguing in Publication

McDowell, Christine, 1953-
    You're not broken : you need to harness your inner power / Christine McDowell.

ISBN 978-1-897453-17-9

    1. Self-actualization (Psychology) I. Title.

BF637.S4M238 2011   158.1   C2011-907693-4

Copyright 2011-08-30 by Christine McDowell
Published November 28, 2011
Manor House Publishing Inc.
(905) 648-2193 www.manor-house.biz

First Edition. 144 pages. All rights reserved.
Cover design: Donovan Davie/Wendy Reyes, based on an original concept design by Wendy Reyes

Printed in Canada.

We acknowledge the financial support of the Government of Canada through the Canada Book Fund for our publishing activities.

Acknowledgements

I would like to thank all my Teachers for their loving kindness, tons of support and buckets of patience. You've all contributed in many ways to helping me see myself in a different light. One Teacher had to keep reminding me that I am a "Unique Piece of Divinity". Yes, I know you told me I was a good student because I did take "Action" where most did nothing and it was because what you said did it *felt* right to me!

Susan Crossman, you're the best! Thank you for ALL your support, for your enthusiasm and most importantly for your *editorial expertise*. Without you Sue, this book would still be collecting dust in the archives of my computer.

Stewart Jones, thank you for believing in me! Without you I probably would be still mucking out stables. You saw and believed in me what I could not ponder and through your coaching, support and understanding I came out on top.

I would also like to thank myself, because without me none of this would have been possible. I want to also say that I am very proud of myself for not giving up on me! I always felt there had to be a better way to live my life. When I remember how I used to be, I shudder as many did when I walked into a room. I am not who I was, so I know that anyone can change and grow. Because, I am living proof!

Everyday I live with love and joy in my heart. Each day I remind myself that I am a Healer, Teacher, Student and a Child of Divinity. I am Compassionate, Giving, Forgiving and Filled with Unconditional Love!

Blessings and love to all

Christine McDowell

You're NOT Broken

Table of Contents

Introduction: My beginning   7

Chapter 1: The day I made a choice.   11
- Live in the Now!

Chapter 2: The power of your thoughts   21

Chapter 3: How your thoughts move mountains   25

Chapter 4: How powerful are you?   29
- What happens next?
- How you can begin to control your thoughts?
- Where does your energy go?
- 3 steps
- What about anger?
- How to cope with anger?

Chapter 5: Where do we come from?   39
- Where do we start?
- Going around in circles.

Chapter 6: Believe in whom?   47
- If you do not believe in yourself, who will?

Chapter 7: What or whom is in your way?   51
- Another piece of the puzzle
- How many pieces are there?
- The questions you need to ask?

Chapter 8: How curious are you?   59
- Those pesky lessons!

Chapter 9: Clear out your clutter!   63
- Do something!
- Who is reflecting what?

Chapter 10: What is the message?   67

Chapter 11: Pinch me! I am alive!   71
- Your own power plant.

Chapter 12: It's okay to love yourself?   79
- Stretching for love.
- Another step closer to love.
- More love stories.

Chapter 13: How grateful are you?   91
- Some more magic

Chapter 14: A movie in the making!   96
- One of many steps
- Creating your dream life

Chapter 15: Are we done yet?   107
- What are Life's Lessons?

Chapter 16: Living consciously?   111
- Five a day?
- My understanding.

Chapter 17: How do you measure up?   115

Chapter 18: What is judgment?   117

Chapter 19: Who is taking care of you?!   119

Chapter 20: Does selfish mean 'No'?   121
- Standing your ground?

Chapter 21: Relationships   127
- What is a relationship?
- Nice to finally meet you!

Chapter 22: Responsibility   131

Chapter 23: Who to trust?   135
- Your past does not = your future!

Chapter 24: As I evolve.   141

My beginning

So you've read every self-help book out there and attended more workshops than anyone you know and still you feel nothing has really helped you figure out what you want to figure out. Deep down inside you know something's missing and you have to keep looking. You can't give up – on yourself, your plight, your life, your soul.

Or maybe things are beginning to make sense to you now but you are nowhere near where you would like to be in life. You can almost touch happiness and love but they are just a little out of reach. Maybe you have a great job and make good money or maybe not and you would like to. Maybe you are married and want out or you want to make the marriage work; maybe you just want to have a superb and loving partner in your life.

Are you a teenager or a college student wanting to know the real truth behind the fuzzy nonsense the "adult" world has been telling you? Who are those people? A gang we call "Society" and we let them tell us what to do, who to be, how to live, and how to die.

Any of that sound familiar? It does to me, because those are all scenarios I've found myself struggling through as I've journeyed to the comfortable peace in which I now live. I've written this book for you because I know that learning how to live a settled life doesn't have to hurt – it can be joyful and fun. Imagine how life would have been if someone told you on your first day alive, "Sit down, fasten your seat belt, relax and *enjoy the ride.*" You might have said to yourself, "Oh fun!!"

It's not like we arrived on Earth with directions showing how to be or find the best loving, caring person possible. Hah! It's more like we were taken to the edge of a pier and thrown into the water with no life preserver. We had a simple choice: swim like crazy or drop like a rock to the bottom. Not knowing how to swim meant that we've had to flop around, gasping for air and eventually clinging to any safe-looking rock we could thrash our way to finding.

And there we've parked, hanging on for dear life, but wouldn't you know, rocks in water are slippery and holding on has not worked. We've slipped on and off a few times and each time reached back for more clinging. At some point we need to let go of what we thought was strong enough to support us and find the power to stay afloat on our own. Giving up and sinking to the bottom of an unforgiving sea is a miserable alternative, which, sadly, some people do choose.

My hopes are that this book will help you achieve your goal of swimming safely on your own strengths so you never give up on your spirit, your life and yourself. Maybe my journey and my insights can give you the perspective you need to stop thrashing and start living. I like to keep things simple, using words everyone understands and stories to which most people can relate. As I've said, your dilemma has been mine too and although what I've experienced may not necessarily sing in your own heart or ring true in your own two ears, that's OK. This is about what worked and works for me. This is about what I have learned and the wisdom I have drawn from it.

I heard an expression a very long time ago that has been a favourite of mine for years and is as true now as it was the first time I heard it: *"When the student is ready, the teacher will appear."* I'm not sure who thought of it or wrote it – there is some suggestion that it is of Buddhist origin -- yet I give them thanks because it helped me to realize that when I am ready to receive new information or a new learning, when I am consciously aware of my need, a teacher will appear. The teacher could be a child, friend, co-worker, or store clerk, it could be a bird singing in a tree, a person honking a horn or even a perfect stranger. I have had many such teachers and I have been told often that I have acted as one myself.

I can be stubborn and pig headed and do not necessarily agree with what someone might say but I think my best quality is that I am a very good student: I question relentlessly, driving some people around the bend with my determination to get as much information as possible. Then after I listen to the information I track down, I check to see if the information *feels right*; if it does not feel right, I let it go. If it does, I take it for a test drive.

When I was younger my belief in people was based on their age, list of accomplishments and their reputation as supposed authorities on diverse subjects. As I matured I realized a lot of that information was hogwash so I decided to take my life back into my own two hands and figure things out for myself. Although some of those lessons were tough and painful, they were invaluable; I learned there was a reason for everything.

Some of what I say may not sit well with you. That being the case just let it go! When it *feels right*, look at it, play with it, do something with it! *Take Action*!

> "All of us, whether or not we are warriors, have a cubic centimetre of chance that pops out in front of our eyes from time to time. The difference between the average person and a warrior is that the warrior is aware of this and stays alert, deliberately waiting, so that when this cubic centimetre of chance pops out, it is picked up."
> ~ *Carlos Castaneda*

"Bigness comes from doing many small things well.
Individually, they are not very dramatic transactions.
Together though, they add up."
~ *Edward S. Finkelstein*

1 The day I made a choice!

My poor parents didn't know what to do and I'm sure they did their best anyway.

My stone-hearted fourth-grade teacher, however, was another story.

If you did something poorly, "Mrs. X" made sure you – and everyone else in the class – were reminded of your inadequacies all the time. The fact that she sat all the people she considered dummies at the back of the classroom was bad enough but the rigorous irritation with which she did it was staggering. We all need to know who the dummies are, don't we? They might be contagious!

Just imagine a fourth grader (that would be a nine-year-old child), sitting with the so-called "dummies", day in and day out. What does that prove to the kid? You guessed it – it proves they're stupid, regardless of the facts of the matter. When I was one of those nine-year old children, Mrs. X did me no favors by defining me for myself in such an unforgiving manner. Going out for recess was joyless since it gave the non-dummies more time to pick on me.

"There goes the dummy."

I'm sure you can imagine how much I loved school.

But let's back up a few meters – how did I, a sweet but slightly unconventional little girl with freckles and white knee socks, get into the Dummy Pen at school? It was a quick slide that started the first week of school. One of my many little problems was that I was a weak speller -- even today I struggle with it. (Thank heavens for spell check!) When Spelling Bee day arrived in those long ago days of blackboards and dusty erasers, I would be scared and worried when it was my turn to stand up. I could not get the letters out of my mouth and it didn't help that I was aware of the timer ticking off the limited seconds available for getting the word right. Before I knew it, time was up and out of the teacher's mouth came the words, spoken with disgust, that brought shame into my little heart.

"You're so stupid. I gave you an easy word."

Here was an adult, a person I was supposed to respect and look up to for guidance, confirming for me that I was a good-for-nothing idiot. What did I know? Children do not know what is right or wrong and think that if an adult is telling them something, it HAS to be true. Educators didn't know any better in those days, I suppose, but it was brutal for me.

Since I could not spell, I guess I couldn't write well either. On one of my compositions I remember seeing in big red pencil, "Very poorly written." This confirmed exactly what I and the others around me had already learned: I was painfully stupid.

To this day, it surprises me how I can so easily remember all the negative things that happened to me as a child. It really left an imprint in my mind and although the story was repeated in other grades, I think Mrs. X was the first one to play the message in stereo for me:

"Stupid. Dumb. Very poor."

As a child I kept finding myself in situations that merely proved what I expected of myself, thanks to the messages the adults in my world had drilled into me. Bad news began to follow me around like a black fog. Children are vulnerable and tend to believe the strangest things – unless guided to know otherwise. Of course, all the kids in school teased me like crazy and I felt no one loved me. I use to cry myself to sleep. It's a wonder I passed elementary school. Well, actually, the reason I got through it all was the fact that I was a wizard in math. When given any mathematical problem, I could figure it out quickly and correctly but for some reason, my super abilities in mathematics were completely eclipsed by my struggle to string letters together in the correct order. Go figure.

Math could not save me from the stone hearted Mrs. X's determination to see me fail and fail I did. Failed Grade Four. How do you fail grade four? To this day I wonder. I was probably the only kid in the entire history of that school that had to repeat grade four. Why did this teacher have it in for me? Was it because one cold day during recess, I ran my tiny little hand along her arm to feel the soft fur of her coat and said "Gee this is so soft"?

"Don't be so bold!" she roared at me. I guess she was a very unhappy person but that's not the message my nine-year-old brain distilled from her behaviour. Again, this confirmed that I was no good. As time went on, I realized that I hated school and I became withdrawn. Because I had learned I needed to fight my way through my childhood, I acted up every chance I got! I was no longer sweet little Chrissy, I was a demon on wheels. I hated everyone and everyone hated me. I did my best to make everyone's life miserable.

After that watershed year, teachers kept telling my parents I was nuts and needed special care. Eventually, my parents saw the wisdom of their words reflected in my behavior and took me to see a shrink in the psychiatric ward of a hospital. There were numerous sessions in that crazy place and I remember sitting on a chair that was so big my feet did not even touch the ground. I remember some nurses walking down the hall towards me as I waited for my turn with the psychiatrist and they all wore an 'oh dear,' look on their faces as they looked my way. At that moment I said, "I'm not nuts and I don't belong here." I hated going there, so much so that I usually vomited in the car on the way to my appointment. People spoke to me like I was an imbecile and that just made me crazier.

With all of these sad little stories playing out in my personal life I also found confirmation of my inadequacy in the media. Since I felt so isolated, T.V. became my reality. I grew up in the late '50s eating dinner in front of the basement T.V. I remember the ads for Barbie, whom I idolized, and I remember how fervently I wanted to look like her, boobs and all. I watched movies about families eating together, playing together and showing they loved each other. There were TV shows about kids just being happy being kids and doing well at everything. This was just another reference point for me as I was growing up and what I saw on T.V. was clearly not happening in my life. In that broken way children sometimes have about things that affect them so painfully, I blamed myself for the imperfect life I was living. I thought I was really bad.

To be honest, I felt a lot like Pigpen in the Peanuts comics. Pigpen always had a cloud of dirt surrounding him and no matter where he went, his head was wreathed in it. There was no escaping my dirty gray cloud either. It seemed to affect my friendships and relationships and working life.

I did not wake up one day and say to myself, "Stop this craziness! I need to get off this merry-go-round and learn how to enjoy my life!" Rather, over a period of about five years, I embarked upon a gradual journey of discovery that started when I asked myself a simple question, "Can I see myself doing the job I'm doing for another five years?" The answer was, no. More questions started to pop up, "Why am I on this planet? What is my purpose?" And, the most powerful question, "Am I happy?" I had to be honest with myself because I knew I was not and I knew I needed to figure this one out most urgently of all.

I guess I was around thirty-five years old when these questions started to come up. At the time my dad was in his early 80's and my mum was in her early 70's, so I realized there would be a good chance I would be on this planet for a while and it might be worth taking the time right then and there to figure out, if I could, how to be happy, all the time.

That's when the games began and I invite you to walk with me through the lessons I learned along the road to discovering that I was not broken and didn't need fixing.

Live in the Now

STEP ONE:

Let's start with something really basic: imagine that your mind is a large chalkboard. Written on the board are all the negative thoughts and situations that prevent you from becoming the person you were meant to be. These are the things that drag you back into the past where they occurred or trip you off into an imaginary future filled with bad things that have not even happened yet. On one side of the board you have a column reserved for all the comfortable things you say to yourself countless times a day:

"I'm not good enough."
"I am a failure."
"What a loser."
"I'm so stupid!"
"What an idiot!"
"How could I be so lame?"
"No one loves me."
"I'm really ugly and will never amount to anything."
"Nothing I want to do ever works out, so why bother?"

You might be tempted to think someone else put those thoughts in your head and you are partially right. Somewhere along the line the messages were planted by someone who said them for the first time. Yet you made the choice, whether it was conscious or unconscious, to believe them. When you believe a thought and keep repeating it to yourself, you give that thought power and you make it your own. You give it permission to set its roots in your mind and, like a weed, it takes over your true identity.

Stop for a moment and think about your life: think about what you think about and then ask yourself, "Are my thoughts chaotic? Is my *life* chaotic? Do I have a lot of angry thoughts and am I surrounded by a lot of angry people?"

Is it possible your thoughts reflect your reality?

As I said, whether consciously or unconsciously, somewhere along the line you gave your thoughts permission to live within you. Some thoughts might stem from what your parents, friends or teachers might have repeatedly said to you as you were growing up. If two people said a similar thing to you, or you heard it repeated over and over again, at some point you might have started to believe it was all true. It's even possible that sometime when you were daydreaming with the TV turned on, your subconscious mind tuned in to a negative comment uttered by a TV character and took it personally. The belief deepened.

We tend to analyze our beliefs and pair like with like so that the negative thoughts match up nicely in matched sets of powerful force. The very act of analysis gives unpleasant thoughts power to grow, and they chip away at our belief in our own goodness. When we don't stop those negative thoughts from taking hold, we are giving them permission to grow, to let their roots take hold so they can flourish and prevent us from thriving as whole, energetic, peaceful people. It almost sounds like a scary movie where all you really want to do is crawl under the bed to hide, yet you are to afraid to do so because there are most certainly other demons under the bed, waiting to tell us more about our own failings.

Ten years as a Lifestyle Coach has taught me well and some of my best teachers have been my clients. I've learned that people do not show up in my life by accident -- they are there to teach me something about myself or to reconfirm something I already knew.

People typically come to see me because they feel they are under great stress. Stress is the root cause of everyone's problems and I think of it as something like the last stop for a train that has passed through many stations marked "Get off now before you get to Stressed". You either get off at the end and finally figure out how to control your stress or sit there and allow more stress to grow like climbing vines over the stationary train, immobilizing it for good.

For my clients, stress comes in many different disguises, followed by many different ailments: they can't keep their focus at work, they are not sleeping at night, they eat too much or too little, they yell at everyone and hate their job, spouse or kids. They get headaches, backaches, stomach aches. The list is endless. Bottom line: their life is chaotic and out of control.

What is the source of all that stress? You guessed it! It comes from all those negative thoughts we allowed to exist on the large chalkboard of our minds. We worry about our futures -- where are we going and how will we get there? We also worry about what we could've, should've or would've done or said to those in our pasts. We think of who we could get even with, because of what they did or did not do, or said or did not say to us. We run through our failed relationships and blame others for what didn't work. It is a constant merry-go-round, circling continuously and making us very dizzy.

STEP TWO:
Now imagine you have the power to completely erase the chalkboard in your head and clear your mind of all thoughts. Pretend there is absolutely nothing on the board; it's blank and therefore your mind is totally blank. *Completely* blank. Knowing your mind is completely blank ask yourself this question:

"Do I have *any* problems now?"

If your mind is truly devoid of thought, your answer should be "No!" How could you have any problems with no negative memories or reminders to shackle you to your past? Doesn't this tell you that you are the one complicating your own life?

Imagine if you cleared your mind of any negative thoughts and focused on living only in the current moment. How much simpler would your life be? Would you experience any stress?

Likely not.

Because clearing your mind of all negative thoughts basically puts you living in "the NOW" and it's what I call "living consciously". When we live in a "NOW" time zone we find great resources of inner power because personal power is based in the present tense, not the past or the future. When we focus on this one moment we are living NOW, we have all the energy we need to *act* more calmly when any situation lands on our plate.

We step back and look at every situation differently -- instead of *reacting* and flying back into chaos, we consciously choose to *act* differently. (And yes, I know that is easier said than done!)

Some things I say might seem too simplistic but keep in mind that the person you are now has been many years in the making. To change your life, you have to change your behaviour and you can only do that one tiny step, at a time. *Change occurs in an instant, but the steps leading up to that instant are the crucial part of the equation!*

The key here is to live consciously in the moment, to become aware of your thoughts and stop them when they get out of control. The key is also to become aware of your actions, so as to cause harm to no-one.

Most people on this planet live unconsciously, with their head in the sand, so to speak. They re-act to the world around them, spewing out whatever suits them, without caring how the person on the receiving end of their words and behaviour feels. It's almost as though people are like, unfeeling, uncaring zombies, dead to the wider world of emotion.

Living consciously means deciding to be aware of your thoughts and behaviours and focusing them in directions that serve you well.

So how exactly can you start to live in the NOW?

Your worries are just thoughts that are out of control, similar to a spoiled kid who chooses to misbehave or act out just to get your attention! It's like when you are in a store and you hear a child screaming her head off because she wants a specific treat NOW. Your thoughts pull the same tantrum repeatedly and for many years you have given in to them, like the tired parent who chooses the path of least resistance. They pull you into the past so you can feel unhappy or angry all over again because of what someone said. They yank you into the future to worry about a presentation you are going give tomorrow. It is amazing how powerful your thoughts can be. You can be as happy as a lark and in an instant your thoughts plunge you into sadness or anger – which, of course, is unhealthy and unnecessary.

I like the Buddhist teaching that thoughts are like water that has an undercurrent swirling around beneath the surface in no particular direction. It pulls us here and there, crashes up against the shore and contributes reluctantly if at all to our desire to reach our destination. Freeing ourselves from thought allows us to navigate easily; it lets us control where we want your lives to take us and lets us choose how we want to feel. We can skim along on calm water or struggle valiantly but unsuccessfully in rough seas. Would you like to be *in control* of your thoughts instead of being controlled by them?

The first step in taking back your power is to be present and conscious of what you are doing all the time. If your mind decides to leave the room and wander off into negative turf, say the word, 'Now'. You can do this surreptitiously inside your head or say it right out loud for the walls around you to hear. Whatever is appropriate or feels right for you is the right way to do this. If your mind wants to go stomp miserably through your past or worry about your future, you need to pull it back to the present moment. And when your mind pulls you away again, drag it back with the word "Now." "Now, Now, Now, ten times, seventy times, whatever it takes, keep saying "Now". But be *kind to yourself* and remember you are trying to calm the waters of your mind.

Your mind has had control over you for a very long time, hasn't it? So now, like teaching your child to tie his shoes or refrain from throwing a tantrum, you need to be very repetitive. Please know that you are not yelling or screaming at yourself to be in the 'Now', you are *gentle* and *kind*. Again, teaching a child to do something is sometimes very frustrating because the child might take a while to learn the task, despite hearing the instructions countless times. It is tempting to become angry and start yelling, which of course entirely frustrates the purpose of the exercise. The poor child would be petrified and whatever was being taught would be lost. So please be kind to yourself. *Speak to yourself the way you want to be spoken to.*

Change takes time, plenty of patience, repetition…and remembering not to forget! Here's an example. You want to be fluent in another language within two years. So you sign up for a course, miss a few classes, do some of the work and practice when you have the time. Is this likely to help you achieve your goal? Or are you more likely to get the fluency you want if you attend all the classes, do all the assignments and practice nearly every day? Learning a new language can be fun, rewarding and exciting. It all depends on the steps you take, the work you put into it and the determination you have to achieve your goal.

Like learning a language, there are things you can do to help you be present in the current moment most of the time. You could put an elastic band around your wrist and each time your mind decides to take a walk without your permission, flick the elastic band. This will quickly bring you back to now. Or you could have the word 'Now' written on a piece of paper on your desktop, so each time you open your computer you will have a little reminder. Stick notes around your house to remind to be present. The easiest thing to do, however, is to say 'Now'. The hardest thing to do is to remember to say it consistently. You may find yourself saying it over and over again. Each day you remember is great and each day you forget, is okay because tomorrow you will remember more than what you did the day before. You must forgive yourself for your own imperfections.

2   The power of your thoughts.

Have you ever been thinking about someone and then they call you, or you walk along the street and they appear? Most people don't tend to equate their thoughts with an outcome. When a friend suddenly shows up on their radar screen soon after you thought about them they might say, "This is really weird! I was thinking about you the other day and now you are here. What a coincidence."

But is it a coincidence? I believe your thoughts create your reality. Imagine sitting in a restaurant ordering a meal. You scan the menu and tell the waitress what you want to order; before long the food is sitting in front of you. How does this apply to the thoughts you hold in your head and the life you are living?

Simple.

Take an event or situation that did not work out the way you had hoped. Can you remember what you where thinking beforehand? What pictures where you holding in your head? What were you saying to yourself? Did these thoughts, empower you or take power from you?

I like to golf and often when we golfers flub a shot, we want to take the shot over. Some of us prepare to retake the shot and say to themselves "I don't want to make the same stupid shot." Guess what? They do! Similarly, someone nervously meeting a prospective client says to themselves before walking into the room, "I'll probably screw this up and lose the sale." Chances are they will. Our results always stem from the thoughts we hold in our head.

Here's a tool you can use to help you change a negative thought or picture into a positive one. When you have a negative expectation about something you can FLIP the thoughts or pictures that accompany it into something more powerful and empowering. Take the negative picture or thought and ask your mind to FLIP it over. If it is still negative, keep saying FLIP. You will see that after a few requests the picture or thought will lose its negative power and slowly start to FLIP over into something more positive. The more you train your mind to FLIP, the easier it will become. Why does it work? Because your mind knows there is an opposite to whatever shows up in it and underneath every negative thought is a positive one. You must keep digging!

Try this: hold a negative word in your head and now say FLIP. If it is still negative, keep FLIPPING and I promise you, your mind will uncover all the positive thoughts buried underneath the negative ones. Remember, practice makes perfect.

Here is another suggestion: you are always in control of your thoughts, whether you realize it or not, so you might as well capitalize on your power and start each day thinking only pleasant, happy thoughts. They can be thoughts about simple things -- feeling the warmth of the sun, listening to the birds or seeing yourself walking in a park or on a beach. Carrying those positive thoughts, positive pictures -- and the feelings they create -- will change the outcome of your day.

This is about YOU becoming familiar with your own thought processes, navigating the world inside your own mind and controlling how you want to think and feel. You do not need to be continually being controlled by your thoughts. If you think this could make a difference in the way you live your life, maybe you might give this a shot for a day or, even better, a whole week.

Another idea for controlling your thoughts is to put a note pad or journal by your bed and before you go to sleep at night write down a few short sentences about how you would like your next day to be. Keep it simple and focus your intention around how you want to feel at the end of an active day. You might also see yourself handling a difficult situation well, without losing your temper.

The purpose of all of these exercises is to hold onto positive thoughts and positive outcomes only -- for you and everyone involved with you. If you have the power to conjure up a person or a parking spot, just imagine what would happen if you put your energy into holding onto thoughts and feelings that empower you? How different would your life be?

Recap - The First Step to Controlling your Thoughts.

Here is what we know we need to do:

- Live in the moment.
- Be consciously aware of the world around us all the time.
- Say NOW to ourselves every time our thoughts start running rampant.
- Be firm with ourselves and if we need to say NOW ten times before we click in, then we do it!
- Stop our minds each time they takes us down the long dark winding tunnel that is littered with negative thoughts.
- Before getting out of bed in the morning or before going to sleep, set an intention of how you want your day to be. Example: I am going to have an amazing, fun loving day. My thoughts and actions are calm, loving and peaceful.

Speak to yourself the way we want to be spoken to.

You are who you have been for a long time. As I have said before and will say again, making any changes within yourself takes time and patience. Do everything necessary to help yourself remember what you need to do daily. Give yourself some reminders by putting little sticky notes with NOW on it. Put one in your car, bathroom mirror, your desk, your computer, wherever you can see it.

Put an elastic band around your wrist and whenever your mind wanders down a dark and unproductive alley, give the elastic a flick to bring you back to the present moment. It is easy to slip back into old behaviours because they are so ingrained in us. And forgetting is normal!

Remember, it's the little things you do **daily** that add up over time to something enormous – like using the Power of your own thoughts to create a reality that makes you jump out of bed in the morning.

Many times people tell me they have heard it all and read it all. Well that is all fine and dandy, but what ACTION are you taking? What are you *doing* to change the things in your life that are not working? Change your thoughts and you change your reality!

"It's the repetition of affirmations that leads to belief.
And once that belief becomes a deep conviction,
things begin to happen."
~ *Claude M. Bristol 1891-1951*

3 How your thoughts move mountains

What do you believe?

Years ago I heard a theory about butterflies. A butterfly could flap its wings in Japan and the effects could be felt in North America. Sounded a little far fetched to me yet for whatever reason it stuck in the back of my mind. Then one day I heard the theory again and being in a different mind space I began to understand the power of flapping wings and flapping anger.

As I began to write this part of my book, I scanned the internet to find out how this theory was defined. It is called the "Butterfly Effect" and some theories where rather complicated, delving into quantum physics which is a bit out of my league. I did find something however which kept it simple and this is what "The 'HYPERLINK" had to say:

"http://www.fortunecity.com/emachines/e11/86/ptlytrue.html#Butterfly "The Butterfly Effect' is the propensity of a system to be sensitive to initial conditions. Such systems over time become unpredictable; this idea gave rise to the notion of a butterfly flapping it's wings in one area of the world, could cause a tornado or some such weather event to occur in another remote area of the world."

What does the "Butterfly Effect" have to do with the topic at hand? If the energy of flapping wings can be transferred across the land, then what power do the energy of our thoughts have? Many people do not believe or understand the power and/or energy our emotions give off but if you've ever lived with someone, you will know the impact their moods have had on you. When you leave the house in the morning after an angry exchange with someone you live with, you carry their negative energy forward with you into other exchanges you have that day. If you've left the house feeling uplifted by a series of cheerful exchanges, your connections with other people during the day will likewise be influenced by the positive energy you carry with you. Likewise, the energy in your mood will set the tone for others who interact with you during the course of a day and this will affect their connections with other people with whom they interact -- and on it goes.

Some people have gone so far as to attempt to quantify the impact of our emotions. An eye-opening book I read by David R. Hawkins ascribes an amount of power/energy to every emotion known to mankind and if you are interested in a detailed account of this topic I highly recommend you read his book, "Power vs. Force". (Published by Hay House, Inc)

David Hawkins states, *"The calibration figures do not represent an arithmetic, but a logarithmic, progression. Thus, the level 300 is not twice the amplitude of 150; it is 10 to the 300th power. All levels below 200 are destructive of life in both the individual and society at large; all levels above 200 are constructive expressions of power.*

In the examples below, a number represents the energy level of the emotion. David Hawkins states that shame, guilt, fear and anger are well below 200 and therefore destructive emotions.

- **Shame** – Energy level 20; losing face, becoming discredited, or feeling like a "non-person".
- **Guilt** – Energy level 30; remorse, self-recrimination, masochism, and the whole gamut of symptoms of victim hood. Guilt provokes rage, and killing frequently is its expression.
- **Fear** – Energy level 100; Fear runs most of the world. Fear limits growth of the personality and leads to inhibition.
- **Anger** – Energy level 150; Anger can lead to either constructive or destructive action. Anger expresses itself most often as resentment and revenge and is, therefore volatile and dangerous. Anger leads easily to hatred.
- **Courage** – Energy level 200; At the level of Courage, an attainment of true power occurs; therefore, it's also the level of empowerment.

- **Acceptance** – Energy level 350; At this more evolved stage, nothing "out there" has the capacity to make one happy, and love isn't something that's given or taken away by another, but *is created from within*.
- **Love** – Energy level 500; Love doesn't fluctuate-its source isn't dependent on external factors. Loving is a state of being. It's a forgiving nurturing, and supportive way of relating to the world.

Again, the Hawkins work shows that thoughts and emotions hold and give off energy and this in turn can be constructive or destructive to yourself, the people around you and ultimately to every life form on this planet.

This is not as far-fetched as it would have seemed a generation ago – today's quantum physicists are actually going beyond the work of the esteemed Albert Einstein and examining these very issues with enormous interest. And, often, with some surprise. If we take the "Butterfly Effect" described above, we can see how one individual's anger has an impact half a world away. By the same token, a peace rally, where everyone behaves in a sincerely loving fashion, is bound to have an impact on the people directly involved and, ultimately, other people the world over. Let's look at two examples.

Imagine first of all a peace rally staged at locations around the world but participants are angry either because they are not being heard or because what they want is not materializing. They are fighting for a cause and typically most peace rallies are *fighting* for something. Fighting for something carries a negative connotation. On that basis, how effective do you think this type of mindset for a peace rally really is?

Case in point – some years ago there was a peace rally to stop President Bush from going to war. Many people around the world where very angry and I still remember seeing the anger coming across in TV reports from the time. I cannot recall seeing rallies at the time displaying any kind of peacefulness, however. The anger each rally produced created more anger and that power was felt by all and resulted in even more anger. It was a vicious circle and the rallies did not move the world any closer to peace,

Let's look at a different example involving the National Demonstration Project to Reduce Violent Crime and Improve Governmental Effectiveness. This group did an interesting study on reducing crime through meditation. On the basis of previous research, it was hypothesized that the level of violent crime in the District of Columbia would drop significantly if a large group of Transcendental Meditation® and TM-Sidhi® participants focused specifically on increasing coherence and reducing stress in that region.

In order to ensure objectivity, a 27-member independent Project Review Board was established to give advance approval of the study's research protocol and monitor the study as it unfolded. The review board consisted of sociologists and criminologists from leading universities, representatives from the police department and the government of the District of Columbia, and civic leaders. On June 7, 1993, the National Demonstration Project to Reduce Violent Crime and Improve Governmental Effectiveness brought approximately 4,000 Transcendental Meditation and TM-Sidhi participants into Washington DC to begin meditating for peace and they continued until the end of the study on July 30 of that year.

After the data was collected and analyzed, Review Board found a 48% reduction in HRA crimes (crimes against a person) in the District of Columbia. To see a detailed report on this study, visit ISTPP Crime Prevention: http://www.istpp.org/crime_prevention.

So what does that show us? In my view, both examples point to the impact positive or negative energy has on other people, near and far. I invite you to take a look at your thoughts and ask if you think your behaviour is having a positive or negative impact on others, on the planet and, most importantly, on yourself.

4 How powerful are you?

One of the biggest gifts you were given, when you arrived on this planet was the gift of "Free Will". You can think and feel whatever you wish. You can choose to be either loving or hateful, to laugh or cry, to be crazy or still, to forgive or not. The choices you have are endless! How you choose to go through this life will determine your outcome, so choose wisely and know that while you might not be able to single-handedly change the world, you *can* set an example others might choose to follow.

I had to get off the treadmill of what I thought was a life and begin to walk my own path before I really started to get this simple lesson. It was not easy because I did not know where my walk would take me. I had managed to cover up my feelings and the rest of my soul with so much nonsense that I could no longer tell what was real and what was fabrication. I almost felt like a seed frozen in the ground, covered by layers of snow. Remember Bette Midler's song "The Rose": beneath the winter snow lies the seed which in the spring becomes a rose.

To step off the treadmill going nowhere and onto a path that leads somewhere, you first have to give yourself permission to take that first unconventional step, to nurture the seed within you that holds all your love, peace and joy. To carry the analogy just a little further, you are like a seed sitting in parched soil: as you feed and water it, your "soul seed" will begin to grow. Without the water, the caring, the love and the light, the seed might die. You may have heard this before: you need to trust in yourself, trust in the Source of all life and trust that you were not put on this planet to live in pain and sorrow: that was a choice, albeit maybe not a conscious one.

Trust is the crucial element that will let you to clear away the dense layers of false beliefs that stop you from growing and the only way to start that process is to ask yourself for permission to do so. This is similar to the permission you might ask if you wanted to use something that belongs to someone. The question always begins with, "May I?" or "Can I?" Why ask for permission when it comes to yourself? Because most of us have lived by rigid rules created by the world around us and being kind to ourselves is not one of the rules; we want to gently change our thinking by involving ourselves more consciously in our own decision-making -- and by respecting the role we ourselves need to play in creating our future.

Just for fun ask yourself "Is it okay for me to be kind to myself?" This may feel silly at first -- I know it did for me. You might hear the answer to this question as a little voice in your head or you might feel it. When I first asked this question, goose bumps ran up and down my arms, and although I did not recognize it as a response, I now know that's exactly what it was.

Over time the voice within me started to find its vocal cords -- or maybe I became a better listener -- and now I ask myself permission to do various things every day. It is a way of respecting myself and when I don't always get the answer I wanted I realize I am on the threshold of learning something new.

What Happens Next?

We need to start taking responsibility for how we think and feel because whatever thoughts and feelings we put out there, they come back to us. Imagine being a radio tower and you are either transmitting or receiving information. Your thoughts and feelings are what you are transmitting outwards and whatever you're transmitting is being reflected back to you.

As you hold a thought in your head, it is then transferred into your body as a feeling. That feeling gives off an energy which is then transmitted out into the universe. Your radio tower is hooked up and running at full tilt.

Your thoughts and feelings are like waves, what goes out comes back in. Here is an example: You've hopefully never said this yourself, yet I am sure you've heard it before, "See, I told you it would not work! I knew I would not get it! I knew I would fail!" The sentences usually begin with "I knew". Which means they had played the scenario in their head and they did it in a way that resulted in a negative outcome.

When you start to take responsibility for your reality, which means taking responsibility for your thoughts and actions, you might find yourself living a happier more productive life. How do you do this? You need to change the way you think and feel! Remember the chalkboard I mentioned earlier in Chapter 1. You need to gradually start controlling your thoughts so you can erase all the disempowering thoughts inscribed upon it and replace them with empowering ones.

How can you begin to control your thoughts?

Imagine that the thoughts rambling around in your head work on the same principal as songs playing in a CD player. You can listen to them repeatedly, hearing the same words and the same tune, you can exchange it for another one or you can turn it off and remove it altogether. Better yet, if the thoughts are harmful to you, you can also pull the CD out of the machine, break it up and throw the pieces away so it is gone from your mind, gone from your thoughts and gone from your reality.

I am making this sound very easy and in one sense it is. You just need to make a commitment to yourself to do whatever is necessary to stop the chatter in your head. Because I have been through it all before and I know that your commitment is key. If you feel you deserve to have a life with peace and happiness then maybe you can find that burning desire to commit yourself to the process.

I had to *believe* it was possible to record a new "Happy, Loving and Positive CD" that would serve me better than the old one. I kept looking at the results my previous thoughts had created, which was pure chaos, and I gently reminded myself that this did not work for me anymore; I truly did not want to take any steps backwards. Most importantly, I did not give up on myself.

Also part of this process, I had to *believe in myself* and know I was worth it. I constantly looked back over my past as a reminder, a very good teacher. Mind you I had a choice, I could have either held everyone responsible for my miserable unhappy life or use it as a guide.

There had been many Teachers who showed up at the right time and, I truly believed and felt right down to my toes, what they where saying to me made sense at some level.

Here's how to start:

Take a pen and write down all the negative things you believed about yourself. Go ahead and write them down on one side of the page. Do not stop till your hand hurts. Now on the opposite side of each phrase write how you now want to begin to think or feel. Here are a couple of examples:

I feel people reject me.	I am accepting of myself.
I am always having to do for others.	I am choosing to do for myself.
I don't think I can do this.	I have the courage to find out.
I am a failure.	I can accomplish many things.
People don't like me.	I love myself.
I have no friends.	I am becoming my best friend.
People say mean things about me.	I speak to myself the way I want to be spoken to.

No matter what you do, you MUST believe in yourself and feel that you are worth it! Eventually others will notice the difference because the energy you are exuding will seem lighter. They may not understand it yet so be prepared for people to ask you what you have done. I used to hear it all the time. Eventually this new way of thinking becomes a habit and I encourage you to review your new thoughts frequently to remind yourself of who you are becoming. Be patient with yourself and keep trying – otherwise you will fall back into your old patterns, feeling not very happy with yourself. You are creating a new dictionary of sorts, a dictionary full of new, productive, and helpful thoughts to replace the old, worn, useless ones.

Where does your energy go?

Most people walk on a path feeling frustrated and exhausted, often forgetting to breathe. Many are full of anger, fear, sadness or guilt, which hinders – or even prevents -- their ability to extend kindness and consideration to others.

To see the impact of this problem, picture yourself in the shallow end of a swimming pool holding a huge air-filled rubber ball. Now, imagine you have to hold the ball under the water. After 60 minutes have passed you are allowed to let the ball go. Your legs are shaky, you are a bit out of breath and your arms feel strained and tired.

Now imagine that huge rubber ball represents all your anger, or any other negative emotion you have been holding on to. When you decided to let go of that anger-filled ball you would also feel shaky, a little out of breath, somewhat strained and tired – and relieved. Why? Because it takes a lot of energy to hold onto negative emotions.

Here's another way to look at this: imagine you have a very large backpack brimful of anger you created because so and so did this or so and so said that. Now, carry that backpack around all day. Don't you think by the end of the day your neck, shoulders and back would be sore? I am sure you've heard the expression when someone's neck or shoulders really hurt, "It feels like I've been carrying the world on my shoulders!"

Is there any wonder why you are so tired at the end of the day? Keeping a rubber ball underwater or walking with rocks in your backpack would slow anyone down! Your energy is being drained from you because it is supporting all the negative thoughts and emotions that you are hanging onto. When will you let the ball go or take off that backpack?

Three step process

The first step in my process is finding out what makes you have an unpleasant reaction. (Why you scream and yell, slam doors etc) The next step is deciding what you want to do differently (a new behaviour/reaction). The final step is to take action: When putting the pieces together, what would it feel like, look like and sound like.

So if you are continually faced with a specific situation that consistently causes you to react negatively, you need to stop "reacting" and instead choose how, exactly, you would like to act. There are people in all of our lives who know exactly what buttons to push in order to make us go crazy...well, find those buttons and change the wiring so you now can act in a more positive, loving way. Is it possible? It is! It all depends on how important it is to you to start being in control, instead of letting people or situations push your buttons.

As with the last exercise, write down all those buttons that people know how to push. It could be what someone might say to you, a parent, sister or brother, yep they know how to get your goat. Write it all down, no matter how silly it might sound to you. If you're stuck for ideas, simply hold off for a while and before you know it a situation will materialize. When it does, write it down.

Now you have an awareness of your "hot buttons", which you did not have before. This is a very good thing. Looking at one thing your wrote, ask yourself how do you now want to act? Remember, every situation that keeps showing up in your life is there to teach you about you. It is not about who is in the event, it is about you and how you act. You can not control the other person, you can only control how you want to behave.

I will give you an example. I love my brother dearly yet growing up with him was no walk in the park. He knew how to get to me and he used every opportunity I gave him to goad me into conniptions. His magic words, "You are just like your sisters!" Boy, that would send me around the bend and back.

Over time I realized it was not what he said or how he said it that drove me crazy, it was the words "sisters". I didn't much get along with them either! I grew up feeling inferior to my sisters and I did everything I could to be as unlike them as possible.

When I began to see this pattern I took a few steps back. I knew I could not be like my sisters and I did not want to be like them. I let go of the judgment involved in the whole situation, held compassion for myself and for them, realized we were all doing the best we could and forgave every one of us for being imperfect!

My sisters were teaching me how I needed to be. I stopped judging myself, and realized I was doing the best I could…and all those family "hot buttons" I had started to slowly cool down. This was not done overnight. My family is still a part of my life yet the "hot buttons" have been disconnected.

What about Anger?

Part of this whole matrix of being stuck in a bad emotional place has to do with our addiction to anger. Anger controlled me for a good part of my life, in fact I think I went to school for anger and passed with honours. Anger was my middle name. It consumed my life and my body. My back, neck and organs became twisted from the tight grip I had on my angry feelings. I was a pretty decent squash player until I could no longer hold a racquet in my hand. Issues I was unwilling to face were being absorbed into my body and damaging it.

Anger or any negative emotion will destroy your body along with your heart and soul, so it is very important you pay attention.

Most of the unease or "dis-ease" on this planet is really based on the negative emotions that we are unwilling to heal and we are bent on holding on to them until our dying day -- which might be sooner than later if you continue letting your ego get in the way. Maybe your only purpose on this planet is to learn to let go of your hatred, anger and dislike for people, things and situations!

I know it's possible – because I did it!

Ask yourself this question: "How does holding on to this anger support or serve me?" If you're living in a body full of headaches, backaches and ulcers, have few friends and you're living a miserable, unhappy life, I suggest to you it's not supporting you, it's destroying you. Do you have to do it that way? Not on your life!

I can remember saying to myself, "Why should I give in? I am not at fault here -- they are! Why do I always have to say I'm sorry?" I know the war dance because I danced it for many years. You just need to decide to let it all go. You can either roll up your sleeves and get down to the demanding work of learning how to do that or you can continue grinding your teeth, losing sleep or being sick. I'm happy with the choice I made on that issue. How about you?

How to cope with anger?

You must believe you are worth it. I can't say that enough! You must believe in you! It is called self-worth and you need to have some of it, or you will not move forward. If you're like me you might also need to get real with yourself and stop playing the victim all the time.

I knew I was an anger puppy and needed to understand where that came from. Part of the discovery was realizing that the anger I held onto was not mine. I had decided to carry everyone else's anger. In order to understand the anger, I needed to look at the events in my life where my anger had caused me to lose control.

The first thing I did was to dredge up a few of the anger-inducing events I had experienced in my earlier years. I realized I had to detach myself from them so I wouldn't keep reliving them. To do this, I put them on an imaginary screen and watched them play out, as though I were sitting in a movie theatre.

I had plenty of popcorn because I knew it was going to be a very long movie! Putting it all out in front of me helped me to stay calm and detached from the emotional aspect of the show. Instead of dropping down into events and letting them swallow me up again, I was able to stay in control; that meant I was able to look for the life lessons.

In every situation, there is a learning and behind each learning there is wisdom. The wisdom can help us to make better choices, so that we do not repeatedly find ourselves in the same situations.

Through this process, I realized I needed to let go of "blame". I had to forgive everyone involved in the anger-inducing events and this ultimately helped me forgive myself for not being perfect. The anger was not about the people in the events, it was about me and how I was choosing to react.

When you live in "victim mode", everything is always about you and the bad things people said or did to you. If you step out of that mentality and detach yourself from the events that made you so crazy angry, it is easier to understand them and, ultimately, easier to shed them. For me, seeing my life play out on a screen helped me to see things from other people's perspectives and helped me realize everything wasn't always about me after all.

Gradually I filtered through the layers of hatred and anger I had carried with me for so many years. It took time and patience for me to let it all go because over time, anger had become my shield and I felt it was protecting me. In actual fact it was pushing people away and keeping goodness out.

In my opinion, too many of us are bouncing around the planet like anger-filled rubber balls. Most people hold onto some level of anger but some hold onto enough anger to cause a natural disaster of epic proportions.

As stated in Power vs. Force by David Hawkins: *Anger can lead to either constructive or destructive action. Anger expresses itself most often as resentment and revenge and is, therefore, volatile and dangerous. Anger leads easily to hatred.*

There is a wick within you that is waiting to become the light of your soul. When this inner flame burns brightly you will feel a magnificent awakening in your life.
~ *Bradford Keeney*

5 Where do we come from?

Here's a fanciful image for you: let's say that way back before you were born you were up in the heavens (wherever that might be for you) having fun with all your buddies. You where happy to be back home finally, getting reconnected with your Source, your Divinity. This might be a fanciful concept for some of you but bear with me.

One day the Master comes into the room and asks, "Who would like to go back to Earth again? There you are in the back of the room growing brighter by the minute, bouncing up and down hoping to be picked. The Master is surprised that you want to go back to Earth considering you had just returned from there.

He asks you: "Why do you want to return to Earth so quickly, when you just got back?" You say, "Well looking back at my most recent journey I can see that I failed miserably at holding compassion for people. I judged everyone and trusted no one. I would like you to send me back so that I can discover how to do this right. Maybe you could give me to parents who fight and hate each other and sisters and brothers who are mean and nasty. Oh, and let me lose a few jobs, marry someone who is highly materialistic, maybe an alcoholic -- no, make *me* an alcoholic. Throw whatever you want my way so that I can learn to be how I am here in the heavens. I want to help make Earth my heaven!

The Master says, "Well, this could be a tough journey and I admire your desire to learn and grow. You must remember, though, that once you pass through this portal you will begin your new life on Earth where you left off before. You will forget that you asked for the journey you are about to embark on. You will forget that you a Unique Piece of Divinity. You will forget about your Guides and

Angels, who will be with you all the way protecting you and keeping you safe. You will choose to live unconsciously and you will forget about your Divinity. You will forget who I am."

You're bold and brassy and you tell the Master, "I'll be fine because I have all of you around me all the time." The Master shakes his head and with his blessing he smiles at you. Poof, your wish is granted. So here you are on Earth now and you've forgotten, haven't you? The End. Now it's the beginning of your new journey. So, are you having fun yet?

Let's say we did have a hand in choosing how our life was to play out, we chose our parents, the ups and downs, the craziness, the good and the bad. Would you stop to wonder why things were not working out? Would you try to figure things out?

What if every situation that showed up in your life was one you had asked for because you felt it would be the best way to learn about yourself? Let's say you were married but the marriage ended in a terrible divorce. You walk around feeling angry, hating men or women, not trusting anyone and hating yourself for getting into that awful situation. You might have said to yourself, "How could I have been so blind? I must have been an idiot! This just proves what a failure I am. I will never love again!

For months you beat yourself up. You see or speak to your ex and your hatred comes out. Oh sure, you might pretend you are okay but secretly wish bad things would happen to him or her. But the negative energy is there all the same.

Now ask yourself, "How does this support you? How does feeling and thinking this way make you a better person? What are you accomplishing for yourself, thinking the way you think and feeling the way you feel? Once again Society has trained you well. You've been trained to see the bad, the negative. You've been told that if your marriage fails you are one big failure. You need years of therapy because you failed to keep things together. Does any of this sound familiar to you?

Now let's look at it all from a different perspective. I want you to think back to the beginning of your relationship, to when everything was working beautifully. Play it all out on that big screen we've rented for the day and look for things that you learned about yourself. Get some popcorn!

I had a client who went through two terrible marriages. Carol was talking about her past marriages and saying how much she hated the men she had married. She spoke at great length about all the bad things they said or did to her. I let her spew on and then asked her how holding onto all this pain and misery was helping her or supporting her. Then I asked her, "Tell me something positive about the first relationship. What did you learn about yourself that you would not have learned if you had not married Joe?"

After ten minutes or so, she was still squirming in her seat, fighting with the idea that something positive could have possibly come from that relationship. As she said, "What could be positive about a man who physically beat me up?" We stuck at it and after a while, and lots of questions from me, she blurted out, "I learned I was worth a whole lot more than how I allowed myself to being treated." Eureka! She found something positive.

Then I said, "Give me something else positive about that marriage." After a few minutes she said, "I thought I was afraid to be on my own and I think I married him because I did not want to be alone. As I am thinking about your question, I realize he was always out anyway, which I guess was a blessing. Anyway, I guess deep down inside of me I knew I would be okay being on my own because after five years of abuse I found the courage to leave."

Without any prompting, Carol looked at me and said, "I found courage because I *did* leave!"

And her second marriage? "What positive things did you learn about yourself?" I asked. "Seems I married a similar guy, he was verbally abusive and an alcoholic," Carol began. "At least in this marriage I only stayed for two years. I used my courage to leave faster because I knew I was worth more."

I looked at her and asked the final question: "As you look back at your past relationships, how do you feel now?" With a big smile on her face she said, "For the first time I feel really at peace with it all, and the hatred and anger I had for those men seems to have lifted. I can't believe how I feel!"

Society has taught us to blame others for our unhappiness and to always look for the negative. In this case that is what my client was doing. She was putting all her energy into hating these men. This depleted her of her own energy, which kept her a slave to the anger which she had held so closely in her heart.

Go back to my story, about how you have decided you wanted your life to play out. Looking at what Carol experienced, her learning might have been to discover her own self worth, and maybe to hold compassion for her husbands, who by the way, were doing the best they could with what they knew.

No situation is ever about the other person in a relationship -- yet we take their actions very personally and react the way society has trained us to react. Detach yourself from the event and look at it from a different perspective. Ask yourself what you are supposed to learn here? What are the positive things you need to learn about yourself so this never happens again?"

Where do we start?

Whatever shows up in your life that sets you off, makes you mad, makes you cry, whatever takes control of you, is where you need to begin. This is the starting point for healing. Healing begins when you get the learning of a situation because it means you are ready to let it go. If you don't get the learning, then the universe will keep sending it back to you until you do.

If there is the slightest truth to my little story about choosing your lessons before you are born into this world, then maybe that's why the universe keeps sending the same difficult situations back to you: you asked for it, now deal with it! If that's not how things work in your own model of the world, then maybe that's just how reality actually does function – and you have to deal with it anyway!

When you live consciously, totally plugged in, paying attention all the time and not allowing your thoughts to pull you here and there, you will start to notice things. You will wonder why things work the way they do. You will wonder why someone said or did something the way they did it. You will wonder why you got lost on a street you know well, you will wonder how a song you were humming suddenly comes on the radio as you're driving your car and you will wonder why the street number of a house you're visiting exactly matches the year of a significant event in your life.

You will see coincidences you hadn't noticed before and you'll wonder if these are clues to some big puzzle you're working on, messages, perhaps, that bring you closer to finding out who you are.

This living consciously is key because you are in more control of your actions, your emotions and what comes out of your mouth. Mind you most feel it safer to live unconsciously. This way they can continue to blame others for the things that go wrong in their life.

I had just received a call from someone who was going on about what this person said and did, and how could they? My old self would have been in there like a dirty shirt, adding more to what was being said. Instead my reaction was, were you in the room witnessing this and who cares what they said or did? That stopped them dead in their thought process because they knew I was not going to play their game.

Let's say angry people start showing up in your space more than once or twice a day. Maybe you know them or maybe they are strangers you observe in the act of yelling at someone else. You might consider stopping and looking to see if there is something there for you to learn. If you are sleepwalking through your day, you will miss the chance to connect the dots of your own existence.

These messages could be trying to get you to pay attention to the anger you've been holding onto. Maybe it is time to let it go and let the anger in you heal. If you find yourself hating a lot of people, then maybe you need to learn to start loving yourself. If you are tired of hearing negative news, turn it off -- or maybe start thinking about positive things. If fearful things show up, maybe you need to understand why you decided to be fearful.

Every situation is there just for you, to teach you about you. I know I keep repeating myself and I guess it is because no matter the amount of times I heard or read something, it never sunk in! AND I know I am unique cause everyone else gets it the first time around!

A friend of mine called me the other day to tell me what was not working in her life. Then I said that precious word, "learning". Her response? "Gee, can't I take a few months off from all this learning stuff?"

" The day you stop learning is the day you die," I said. "I didn't know you wanted it to happen so soon!" We both laughed.

Going in Circles

I spent years looking for love in all the wrong places. I felt I was on a merry-go-round, circling the park at very high speeds. My life was falling apart, or at least that's what I thought. Eventually I transferred onto a new path and learned to give myself permission to love myself.

This too, I mention many times throughout the book. Loving yourself is so very vital to your existence, to your peace of mind and happiness. It is now a part of my essence, my mantra and part of who I am now! I will tell you later how I learned to love myself but I introduce the concept now to let you know it is possible and it's not flaky.

Recap:

It is easy for me to tell you what to do and I recognize it may not be so easy for you to do it. It really does get easier. If someone is ranting, raving and spewing nasty words at you, do not add fuel to their fire. And (easier said than done) don't take any of it personally: it's their own stuff that's driving them crazy and it's not about you. You just happened to be in the wrong place at the wrong time, so to speak. There is still a learning in there for you.

You could consider they might be having bad day: maybe someone cut them off while they were driving to work or they lost their job, or possibly their spouse walked out on them. You don't know what's going on in their life. So when someone starts to spew at you, take a deep breathe and hold it. Then see if you could hold a little compassion for them.

You have other options as well. You could ask them, point blank, if they are angry at you or even kindly ask if they are having a bad day. Maybe you could ask them if there is something you could do to help them out. Just do not react. Do not get pulled into their chaos. Simply say, "I can see you are busy and I will come back later."

When you discover who you are, what you like and don't like and what kind of behavior you are willing to tolerate, your journey begins to take on a new light. You once had given your power to others to control you and now you have all the power back into your hands.

The power you seek is living in the present moment, being conscious 100% of the time. I am committed to doing whatever it takes to help me be present, conscious and aware. One thing that has helped me is I've started looking around and noticing the things I appreciate. On the golf course I will say, "I appreciate the sun and the cool breeze. I appreciate the green grass and the tall trees. I appreciate how well I hit my shot. I appreciate being here and playing golf." I think you get the picture.

When I am standing in line at the grocery store or at the bank I look around and note what I appreciate. When driving and not wanting to fall into another trance, I rattle off what I appreciate seeing as I drive by. The more things you appreciate might show up in your life more often and you are living more consciously.

You must master the trick of living in the present moment or you run the risk of getting continually pulled back into your past, living it as though it were happening all over again. You will be in danger of being consumed by the negative past events and you might be blinded by the anger, hatred and fear that festered there. You might be so debilitated by this negativity that you can't even begin to pull yourself back out to safety.

The bottom line is, your life is about learning how to love, honor and respect yourself. Speak kindly to yourself, give yourself a hug and treat yourself with respect. I often talk about loving, honoring and respecting yourself. These are all vital to your happiness and joyful existence on this planet.

'Imagine that every person in the world is enlightened but you. They are all your teachers, each doing just the right things to help you learn patience, perfect wisdom, perfect compassion'
- *Buddha*

6 Believe in whom?

Way back when I was married, I drove my husband around the bend because I could never make up my own mind. I would always ask people what they thought I should do about one situation or another. I guess I was afraid of making my own decisions. As strange as it may sound, I really wanted other people to make decisions for me, for lurking in the back of my mind was a big fear of making the wrong decision. If I made the wrong choice, then that would have meant I had failed -- and that scared me.

Asking other people what I should do was quite a logical to me: if they made the wrong decision I could easily blame them; they would look like a fool and I would get off scot free. I am sure some people saw through my silly antics and thought I was foolish anyway. I learned eventually...

Years later I discovered that people whose opinions I sought could actually destroy the future I was trying to create. While we typically seek advice from someone whose expertise we respect, or someone who is older and, hopefully, wiser, they are not necessarily better equipped to give advice than we are. And while most people want to see others succeed, there are those out there who are envious, and they may not give the kind of reliable feedback one would hope to receive.

When I was younger I did not believe in myself or even knew that it was something I needed to do. The word intuition was foreign to me. Today, I am still a work in progress and while I still second guess myself from time to time, I have a much greater faith in my own judgment than I ever thought possible.

> I will not let anyone walk
> through my mind with their dirty feet.
> - *Mahatma Gandhi*

If you do not believe in yourself, who will?

As a child I was loud and forever in peoples faces. Yet deep down inside I was one scared little kid. I grew up fearing failure and the thought of making a wrong decision would be catastrophic, because then how would people see me.

Then one day I read about Thomas Edison. Someone had asked him why he did not give up after failing hundreds of times to invent a light bulb. Edison had replied that he had never actually failed, he had simply learned a new way not to do it!

Well, I had to think about that! What he said piqued my attention. Edison was putting a different spin on failure. He was saying failure was a good thing. How could this be? How could failing be positive?

With the help of Thomas Edison I began to think differently about failure. Failure started to become my friend instead of my foe. I started to realize there is no right or wrong decision. Just go for it and make a decision and if it works out the way you wanted, great. If not, then make another decision. Learn from what doesn't work and use those learned lessons to gain more wisdom. What a concept!

Remember the game show, "The Price is Right?" Bob Barker would ask contestants to "Pick a door. Is it Door #1, Door #2 or Door #3?" Behind one of those doors they were going to find either an amazing prize, a not-so-amazing prize or a dud. Contestants would look out into the audience for advice and you would hear different voices urging the selection of different doors. Confusion swept over contestants' faces at these moments. Oh what door to pick?

Life is similar to that game show. Questions run through your mind as life's choices appear before you: "Do I take Door #1, Door #2, or Door #3. Then we run around to people asking for their advice. We are always looking for a short cut or a sure bet or, at the very least, some confirmation that we've picked the right door.

Note to reader: It does not matter what door you pick and there are no short cuts because each door will eventually lead you to the next one. And behind each door is a powerful lesson. Wrapped up within that lesson is the wisdom you seek which will help you to continue of your journey a little lighter and little wiser.

When you live consciously in the NOW, you'll notice when history repeats itself. Maybe you might catch yourself saying, "Why does this keep happening to me?" Either you can choose to stop, look, listen, learn and then choose wisely, or you can continue living in ignorance of the possibilities available to you.

Don't be afraid of the learning. I've had many teachers bring me the same message: "No matter who or what shows up in your life, Christine, they are there for you and requested by you to help you discover who you are." The importance of this message took some time to sink in but now I view all events – whether good or bad – just another opportunity to grow.

A friend of mind said he used to think his life was about getting up in the morning, going to work, coming home, eating dinner, going to bed and then starting the whole process over again the next day. But he noticed that when you stop, look and listen, he got a different perspective about his life and he become curious about what really made him tick.

That perspective is invaluable. When I started to look at what was happening around me I realized I neither knew nor understood myself very well. My relationships with people were inconsistent and unsatisfying. I realized I had surrounded myself with meaningless relationships, which created more stress in my already stressful existence. As I became more accepting of myself, I began to wonder if I actually accepted the people around me.

That's an OK question. I believe that understanding ourselves requires that we get out of our own way or better yet, step outside of the boxes we create for ourselves. Go ahead, lift the lid off that box of yours, get the ladder and climb up to the edge. Look over to the other side. If you are feeling very brave, just step out of that box you called home, the place you thought was safe, and take a big breath and jump. Trust me, you will land on your feet.

When you are standing there on your own two feet, you might feel a little weak kneed, and there is a good chance you might fall on your rear end -- and that's okay. What is really cool is that you're making your own choices based on your needs, not what the people and institutions around you need you to need!

> There are two ways to slide easily through life:
> to believe everything or to doubt everything;
> both ways save us from thinking.
> ~ *Dalai Lama*

7 What or whom is in your way?

When you hold any amount of anger or blame, or see everything as negative, your ability to experience any growth in understanding is almost impossible. Unfortunately, we live in a society that has trained us to see and think negatively. The media surrounding us -- including the film industry and the news business -- show us what we are *missing* and they paint a picture of how we should look (but do not).

I invite you to step out of your box and start looking for the positive side of things: when you do, you will see a learning, the areas within yourself that you need to personally improve or work on.

A repertoire of bad habits does us a disservice and we need to create a new bank of good habits. One great way to start is to retrain yourself to react well to a negative situation. Get into the habit of saying, "What's great about this?" It might strike you as naïve but you'll be amazed at what happens when you take a big step backwards and look at the situation from a different perspective.

Another way to look at this is to imagine seeing the negative situation playing out on that trusty movie screen of your mind. You must remember to detach yourself emotionally from what was being said or done to you.

When you get to the end of the movie, ask yourself again, "What's great about this? What can I learn from this event that will help me to be a better person?" Look for the goodness in EVERYTHING. I promise you that there is a learning underneath it all and it will bring you closer to understanding the goodness that lives within you.

Another piece of the puzzle:

I feel the two missing links in our desire to create a chain of success in our lives are the lack of trust in ourselves and the lack of belief in ourselves. Without those two links, managing our lives is like trying to drive a four-wheel vehicle using only two wheels: it's impossible to get very far. It also leads to a feeling many people have of being stuck in the same old rut and not moving successfully in any direction.

But we can't create any forward motion until we begin to understand ourselves and become leaders in the effort to know we are trustworthy and believable. That process requires us to discover the truth about ourselves and the world we live in, and one of my goals in writing this book is to show you how to do this, how to begin to trust and believe in yourself.

Look at your life as a large puzzle. On the cover of the puzzle box you see your picture, so you know how the puzzle should look when it's complete. Some of us want to try and finish the puzzle as quickly as possible – but they forget to read the fine print on the bottom of the box that says:

"Do not get discouraged if you cannot complete your puzzle as quickly as you would like. It could take you a lifetime of learnings to determine how easily all the pieces fit together. Be patient with yourself and trust that all will fall into place at the appropriate time."

At least that is what is written on my box.

This is what I've figured out:

As you learn and grow, you receive new wisdom and another piece of the puzzle snaps into place. Take for example a child who is curious about the red glow of a lit burner. You might tell the child that it is hot and warn them to not touch it. Some children, being very curious, might not listen. They put their hand on the burner and quickly feel the pain. Do they learn not to do this anymore? What do you think their learning would be? Not to do it again? Another piece of the puzzle drops into place and they are another step closer to understanding who they are.

This is a big job. Piled neatly on the table are 4000 puzzle pieces and since that's a lot of pieces, you might have figured out a strategy to get started (some of us do). So you separate out all the pieces that have one flat side because you know they represent the outer edge. You work away and get the outer edge of the picture in place. Great job! But then you glance over and see all those unsorted pieces. A feeling of overwhelm rushes over you as you realize you have a long way to go before your picture is clear.

How many pieces are there?

You are on an amazing journey and I hope by the time you get to the end of this book, you will know it to be true. Your journey is a vast road full of information and knowledge that brings you closer to your spirituality. Long ago, I heard that "I am a spirit living a human life" and up until that time I had thought I was a human being just trying to live. And doing a poor job at that.

As I started my life's journey of discovering how to trust and believe in myself, a lot of new information came flying at me. Some of it made sense but most of it made my head spin. Even the ideas that made sense scared me a bit because I had been living with my head in the sand and it was all new to me. Eventually I shifted into another mode and thought I was either losing my grip or was actually much less intelligent than I wanted to be because I could not understand most of the concepts that were streaming my way. No one told me this journey of self discovery would be easy or hard, so I did not know what to expect -- or even how long it would take for me to become more at peace with my life.

The result was that I was often ready to give up. I wanted to go back to my old ways of thinking because this new journey was way too much work for me. And some of it was pretty far-feteched, when I measured it against my old ideas. I became frustrated and very demanding of myself, which is not exactly the best way to behave, especially if you want to start to make changes in the way you think or feel.

At times I felt I was in a losing battle with my old thoughts. Most days they seemed to be winning and on those days I gave up on myself and fell into that trap of beating myself up. This was an old behaviour and the old recordings started to take hold, "How stupid can I be? Have I got sawdust for brains? I will never get this and I will be just another big failure!"

There were occasional odd days where a little ray of light would shine in. I would be sitting feeling very low because nothing was working and then something would happen, either a helpful new thought would come into my head, or the phone would ring bringing good news or someone would give me a hug. Somehow it would feel like someone was trying to tell me something and that I was okay and just needed to be patient.

Eventually I stopped fretting, stressing and wondering if I were doing everything right or missing all the important messages. Eventually, I began to trust that all this new information would one day make sense to me and a wonderful thing happened: I stopped expecting miracles. I eased up on myself and allowed myself time to grow into all this new information. It was similar to trying on a new pair of shoes. You need to ease yourself into them and allow the leather to take on the shape of your foot before they can begin to feel like a second skin.

My frustration came from trying to put that pile of unsorted puzzle pieces together in one sitting. I was the type of person that needed to know exactly how to create change and how to do it right the *first* time around. Anybody else out there like that? I was so afraid that if I did not understand this new way of thinking, if I could not figure it out pronto, I would be lost forever. I had to get it, understand it and absorb it at any cost. Hell, I just left a six figure income, so I'd *better* get it – and fast! Can you just imagine the pressure I was putting on myself? I was doing a good job of driving myself crazy.

Funnily enough, around about the time I was at my highest level of frustration I started seeing or hearing the words "believe" and "trust". It would show up in a book I was reading or I would turn on the radio and there would be a song about believing. I knew somehow they were messages for me because they would pop up when I needed them most. Trusting in myself and trusting in the information being presented at some point it would all come together and make sense. And that is what faith is about.

So I lightened up and stopped being so hard on myself. I stopped expecting answers right away. And my journey seemed to magically lighten up. I was getting more 'ah ha' moments where another piece of my puzzle would fall into place. It was a great feeling. One evening, as I was flying home after an out-of-town workshop, I noticed how relaxed I felt, even though it had been a long week of demanding personal work. Everything I had understood was running around in my head and I just sat back and watched it play out. In that moment I realized the more I let go of my anger and fear, the less stressed my body felt. The less I stopped pushing for things to happen the more at peace I became. The light at the end of the tunnel was getting brighter and brighter and my journey was getting lighter and lighter."

The questions you need to ask?

Do you ever wonder why you get confused about the simplest thing? Do you ever ask yourself, "Why can't I trust me?" I used to know that feeling well! Here's what I figured out for myself and it might help you too. As a child, I grew up looking to others for guidance, for answers. I would ask questions of my parents, teachers, clergy, and typically any authority figure who I thought should have the insight I was seeking. As a highly curious child I would ask so many questions I would eventually be told to stop and go play in the traffic. Incidentally, this is not a good thing to say to a child. It shut me down. It was almost like turning off the light and years later it became a struggle to find the switch to turn it back on; for some people that fumble for the switch can take a lifetime.

But asking questions was a life-long habit of mine which I supplemented with a tendency to ask for a lot of opinions. I liked to look for a short cut. But over time I discovered that there are no short cuts to learning about yourself. If you want to know who you are you've got to get down into the trenches, roll up *your* sleeves and get to work. Otherwise, you can continue asking for directions from someone else – but just realize that what's right for them might not be at all appropriate for you.

Here is a question for you: Do you want to start living your own life or continue living someone else's?

Imagine a mother telling her child to stay away from the beach. Being a child, her daughter never questioned the directive or even dared ask 'why not'? She just did what she was told. Years later, her friends invited her to go to the beach with them. She began to feel uneasy and somehow she knew this feeling was connected to 'going to the beach' so she turned down the invitation. Her friends thought she was crazy. They were her friends and felt she was missing out on a good thing -- so they literally dragged her reluctantly along with them.

Finally the girl stood on the beach with the sun on her face, her feet sinking into the sand, the water washing over her toes, and she felt like she was in heaven. She looked out over the horizon and breathed in the beauty of the scenery, feeling goose bumps run all over her. She wondered why she had never gone to the beach. She vaguely remembered her mother telling her to never go to the beach. But she didn't remember why. At this point in her life, the girl didn't really care, she was just happy her friends had dragged her along. In drops another piece of her puzzle.

No matter how well-intentioned people are, their efforts to shield us from errors in judgment stop our growth process. We need to figure out for ourselves what works and what doesn't work, what feels right and what feels wrong. If we don't go through this process, we miss out on opportunities to learn more about ourselves, especially about our strengths and weaknesses. Then we can decide if we want to strengthen our weaknesses.

If you wanted to build a solid home, you would need to start by laying a strong foundation. Learning who you are is like building your own home, one brick at a time. Homes that have taken a long time to build, where a lot of thought and care have gone into the planning, are homes that stand proud and strong.

Each step you take, each brick you lay, is part of your journey, your discovery of yourself. Each brick, each step, builds your confidence -- and in time your self-esteem shines through, giving you the courage to take another step. It is important to remember that every action causes a reaction and you must learn to take responsibility for yours actions.

Taking responsibility is vital to living in harmony with all that is around us. When you don't want to take responsibility you just point fingers and blame. Remember when you point a finger, three are pointing back at you! Somewhere in the process, you are responsible.

An example of taking responsibility: Tom was driving and not paying full attention to what was going on ahead of him. He ran into a car that had stopped to let a bus pass. Tom jumped out of his car, yelling and screaming like a lunatic, and took on the poor elderly lady who was driving the car in front of him. She was already a bit shaken up from having been hit from behind and she did not need Tom's verbal attacks.

This is just one example of someone blaming another for their mistakes. We live in a society which does not teach kindness. The attitude is, "I'm right, you're wrong and I can prove it!"

Recap:

We started this chapter talking about the importance of believing in yourself and trusting yourself and the only way to do this is by being open to every opportunity that presents itself to you. You need to embrace those opportunities and learn from them. Take the time to discover new things about yourself, to uncover your hidden talents, and to unleash the wealth of information that has been stored away in your heart, soul and mind.

Remember you are building YOUR home, one brick at a time. If you do not like the floor plan, you can change it. If you want to change the colors, you are free to do so. You do not need to wait or ask someone's permission, just do what *feels right*. Learn from what does not work. Look for the wisdom. Each step, each brick, brings you closer to knowing and understanding who you are. How powerful is that!

You did not come on this planet wrapped up in anger, pain and fear. You were wrapped in love, filled with peace and harmony. You were given 'Free Will', to make choices, to decide for yourself what is right or wrong. Society has done a very good job of numbing you so you don't feel that love and don't accept that you have many hidden talents and insights. It's time to wake up and take back your power, open your eyes to who you are and change what you need to change within yourself, so that you can now allow the love to wrap you up once again, bringing you peace and harmony.

One brick at a time.
One step at a time.
One day at a time.
Everything in it's own time.

8 How curious are you?

A baby takes its first steps on wobbly little legs and as it struggles forward there is no doubt -- in the beginning at least -- that it will fall flat on its rear end at some point in the process. As soon as Baby hits the ground, he or she struggles to stand up again. Do you think a baby sits and reflects upon its next move or ponders the merits of not getting up at all? Can you image a world where babies stopped trying to get up after their first shocking bum drop?

Babies are just plain curious and they rarely give up. Each step they take, each item they stick in their mouth, each door they open, brings them closer to understanding what they like and don't like. This is self-discovery in its simplest form.

Where did our curiosity go? Why have you stopped trying to figure out who you are and what makes you tick? What excites you? What gives you a reason to jump out of bed feeling joyful? Do you know who you are? Have you ever asked yourself these questions?

When I ask people to tell me who they are I find that most will either tell me about their work or simply look confused. People typically define themselves by what they do, where they live and what they have. What many have lost sight of is that we are not the things we collect or own and we are not our jobs – we are much more than that!

Many of us have gotten so caught up with the race to own more stuff that they truly don't have the time or patience to find out who they are. They would rather spend time trying to figure out how to use the latest gizmo or read up on the object of their latest desire.

Ads on TV tell us who we are not and who we need to become in order to be happy and feel successful. So we try to lose weight and get a facelift, a nose job or a boob job. We buy the best clothes, a big house or a fancy car. We create a lot of debt and live with the stress. We take on more than we should because we are busy proving that we are super people juggling ten things at the same time and running constantly all day every day.

It seems as though people are running away from who they are. People hide behind their jobs. Some like to be crazy-busy because otherwise they would need to listen to the voices in their head. They would look in the mirror and have to figure out who the masked person looking back at them was? No, not Zorro!

Here's a test: Imagine being stranded on a desert island with a bunch of people. No one knows who you are nor do they care what you owned or how much money you have because on the island, it is all useless. Now if you had a case full of money that could come in handy to help start a fire. You are all on the same playing field, stranded, scared and hungry. No one cares where you came from. All they want to know is how can you help them to survive on the island?

So, what are your talents? Do you know? As I mentioned before, babies are plain curious. In a way you need to have that same curiosity as a baby. You need to start finding out what you like and what you don't like.

When you bring back the curiosity, you would be one step closer to seeing who you are. Here are some questions for you:

What do I like/love?	What don't I like?
What makes me happy?	What makes me sad?
What's important to me?	What do I not care about?
What excites me?	What depresses me?
What behaviours could I change?	How would I like to behave?

These questions will help shed some light on who you are.

When you begin to understand what is important to you, what makes you happy, you begin to feel differently about yourself and you start to look at things differently. You realize you are in control and no longer being controlled by others. You find respect for yourself and can be happy knowing that doing the best you can is just perfect. The CD 'must be better than that' begins to lose power over you.

Those Pesky Lessons!

Part of discovering who you are is finding out why you get angry or sad, where your fear comes from and what drives it, and what other emotions make you act like a crazy person. As discussed in a few Chapters, negative emotions can be exhausting. Some days you might feel as though you've been on a roller coaster ride, feeling good one minute and upside down the next.

Like anything in life, too much of something is not good for you. One more drink might do you in, one last bite might make you feel like you are going to explode. Too much anger can be deadly for you and for the person on the receiving end. Fear can be like concrete shoes preventing you from moving forward. Sadness can lead to depression. Hurt can paralyse you.

You can tame the emotions that have a terrible hold on you, and like the taming of a cat or dog, this takes time with plenty of patience. The closer you get to taming your unruly emotions, the closer you get to living a peaceful, joyful life. And, yes it is possible!

Emotions teach us about ourselves. Fear tells us what is safe and what to avoid or pay attention to. Anger tells us how far someone can go before they push up against your boundaries. Then it is up to you to decide how angry you want to get in order to let them know how their words or actions have driven you around the bend. Sadness gives us permission to let go and hurt can teach us to say 'no'.

Many would like us to believe that emotions are a bad thing and too much of something can be overwhelming. When you have emotions under control they can become your ally. You need some fear to protect you and keep you safe. Anger is not about how big a bite you can take out of someone, it is a little nudge to keep you honest with yourself. Sadness lets you know it is okay to cry and we know we need to give ourselves sometime to heal.

Society has helped us believe that we need a lifetime of therapy to get rid of our anger and if that does not work, then bring on the drugs. Numb us to the point that we can no longer feel what we need to feel in order to heal what needs to be healed within us. You need to be at a point in your life where you've had enough. Where you're tired of screaming and yelling, tired of crying and not trusting, fed up with all the confusion and exhausted by trying to keep up.

YOU are the most important person on the planet and without you there would be nothing. Do you get what I mean? Without you, nothing would exist! Understanding yourself is your Number One priority! Respecting and honoring yourself is your ultimate goal. I want you to have a new mantra and say it with meaning, 'I'm doing the best I can.' Please remember, "One step at a time, one minute at a time, one day at a time". Patience, patience and more patience.

> "We have what we seek. It is there all the time, and if we give it time it will make itself known to us."
> ~ *Thomas Merton*

9 Clear out your clutter!

To start the ball rolling, within yourself, you need to doing something that is different from what you would normally do. Here's a simple, but profound example; Around the time I started getting all these new ideas and thoughts about myself, I decided I was going to paint the inside of my house. Before I began I had to clear out the china cabinets, remove all pictures from the walls, move my plants and cover the furniture. When I had finished, the rooms and walls were bare and I remember noticing that as I walked around the house, the air felt lighter.

I painted the walls in new colours, full of comfort and depth. When all was done my house felt more alive and funnily enough, so did I. Most of my stuff stayed in the boxes and did not make back on the walls or on my shelves. They found another home to go and clutter up.

Sitting in my living room and admiring my colour scheme, I wondered where I got the strength to paint all those walls and ceilings. I giggled and shook my head as the pain of complaining muscles shot through my back and neck; my arms felt like they were going to fall off. What an exercise! I had a new house and a lighter me. What a relief, I did not need to surround myself with things any more. *The clutter was gone!*

The other big relief came from realizing I didn't need to fill those empty spaces on the walls and shelves. Nor did I want to. It's been years now since I bought any kind of dust collector because every time I've been tempted, I've first asked myself how the item in question was going to enhance my life. When I became conscious of what I was doing, I stopped clutter from returning to my home.

Next I moved on to my clothes closets. If there was something that I had not worn in a year, it was packed off to people who needed it more. When I was done. I found that my clothes where no longer squished together and I could find what I wanted quickly and easily.

As I took the time to clear the clutter from the basement, the laundry room and every other room in my home, it seemed as though my mind was also becoming clutter free. I was amazed at how much clutter I had amassed and I guess at some level it had a protective function -- from what I do not know. It was, however, clouding my vision and taking over my space.

Do something!

Jumping from clearing the clutter to changing your life might seem like a tall order for some people.

The reason so many people fail to change themselves is that they try to do 10 things at once. This is called the super person syndrome and it causes many people to give up. The only way to create effective change is to pick one issue and work with it ONLY!! Trust me – I've tried doing it the other way and it just doesn't work. Crazy time!

There is no right or wrong way to start effective change to support your new focus on a happy life -- just do *something*. Take one thing from this book and practice it daily. For permanent change you need to be consistent with yourself otherwise you will flip back to your old stuff. Here is an example: Lets say you wanted to change the way you part your hair. You want to part it in the middle of your head. When you first try to do it, will it stay? No. If you're highly committed to changing the location of your part you might consider getting gel and wetting your hair many times before it behaves. If you stop doing what needs to be done, then your hair will just fall back to its previous location. Remember, everything will stay the same unless you consciously decide to take a different route.

Please don't try to be Rocky and pick the hardest thing first to change. Some of us want to make up for lost time and take on way too much. You know those people who make a New Years Resolution and want to lose 20 pound in one week. They join a fitness club and workout like idiots. After day one they are burnt out. They had set themselves up to fail. It is as though they wanted to prove to themselves and the world that they are useless and nothing will help them other then years and years of therapy.

Go out and buy yourself a journal. It does not need to be a fancy one. Just something that has a bunch of papers secured together. I know what you're thinking, "I can't write. I don't write. Can't be bothered. Boring!" Well if you want to make changes you need to take ACTION because without it, you will stay stuck in your muck!

Before your shut your mind, consider this: If writing your thoughts and feelings could help you understand yourself better and help you figure out what you need to change within you, would you do it? It's the action you take that will start your wheel turning.

I'm sure this information is not all new to you. Sometimes we need to hear or see something 50 times before we decide to act. Why is that? Maybe we are not ready to turn the page. Maybe we do not have a burning desire to change. Maybe we just want to read and continue to do nothing. That's okay -- just recognize that this is the choice you are making at this time and honour it.

I know some people are just waiting for someone to tap a wand over their head or ask Scotty to beam them up and transport them somewhere else. Wouldn't that be nice? No! Where would the fun be in that? You would miss all those amazing lessons!!!

Since this is not a fairy tale let me share a secret with you. The only thing you need to do to begin to make changes in your life is to "TAKE ACTION." Stop sitting on the fence! Stop telling yourself this is way to complicated and you don't have the time! If you want happiness and joy in your life, then make the time!

Who is reflecting what?

I believe that the people who are in our lives are a reflection of who we are. Most of us do not consciously know who we are, so let's walk through an interesting exercise that will help us find out. Pick a person you know who you are not crazy about. It could be a parent, sibling, co-worker or an ex-friend. Write down all the things you don't like about this person. Maybe you don't like how they look or maybe how they talk to you which drives you batty; perhaps they have a behaviour you dislike. Whatever comes to mind about this person, write it down and keep writing until you have at least 20 complaints.

Now, look at what you have written and ask yourself -- and be honest here -- if this is how you see yourself – do you actually behave the way you have portrayed your disagreeable acquaintance? If you want the truth, ask a friend – a close friend whose opinion you trust. Show them what you have written and ask them if this is how you behave. Be prepared for a shock and forgive your friend for their honesty if what you hear is not want you want to hear.

I remember doing this exercise and writing about someone I really disliked. The way they spoke to me angered me. They teased me, made fun of me and always wanted to be the centre of attention. Well, surprise, surprise. When I had written this down, and a whole lot more, I refused to believe that this was how I behaved. I went to more than one friend and asked their opinion and they all said I was *almost* like that.

Did I want to believe them? Was I hurt by their honesty? Did it take me a few weeks before I wanted to even see these people or even speak to them? Yes, yes and yes. I had asked people for their honest opinion and instead of thanking them, I was angry with them. I don't care who you are it's not easy finding fault with yourself and then asking someone else to confirm it. But as difficult as we may find it, that can lead to positive changes.

10 What is the message?

I often say to my clients, "Imagine everyone you are in contact with is walking up to you carrying a silver tray. On that tray is a gift for you - - maybe not the type of gift you expect, but a gift nonetheless. What type of gift? One that can bring you closer to loving and honouring yourself, one that can bring you a step closer to knowing who you are. The question is, are you conscious enough to receive it?

Example: A few people keep telling you how much they hate themselves or they hate someone else. Maybe you hear the word 'hate' a lot. You turn on the radio and a song features the word, or it stands out as you skim through the newspaper. The question you could ask yourself is this: "Do I hate myself?"

Your initial thought might be, "No, of course I don't hate myself!" Then ask this question, "Do I love myself?" You can't love yourself one day and hate yourself the next but claim you love yourself all the time. Get real! You either love yourself 100% or not. You can't be half pregnant.

Let's work with that concept of percentages. Do you hate yourself 5%, 10% or 50% of the time? It it's any more than 0%, you need to work on this. Get out a notebook and write at the top, "What do I hate about myself?"

As things come into your mind, jot them down. Don't be shy, write a few pages, and don't be surprised if you go off topic or lose the thread of what you are doing. It's OK if what you are writing doesn't make sense. Just keep doing it because in the end you will discover the parts of you that need healing.

Sometimes it happens that someone writes for a few pages but doesn't come to any "Ah ha!" conclusions about what they need to do. If that happens to you, then stop and turn to a fresh page and start jotting down ideas for how you could start loving yourself. What are some of the things that you could say to yourself or do for yourself that could bring you closer to being your best friend?

Is anger an area you want to work on? If so, look for alternatives to anger – what could you do instead of staying stuck in an angry mindset? When you experience anger, what about walking out of the room before you lose control? Or if you are talking on the telephone, why not stop the conversation and commit to calling back when you're calmer before you react badly. Yes I know, easier said than done!

To begin to heal you need to acknowledge the hatred or anger within you. The next step is to come up with a list of alternative ways to act – so you are not always reacting. People who do this usually get relief – either the negative behaviours stop or the people themselves stop showing up in their lives.

Why? Because you got the learning you needed to heal the part of you that was sitting in anger or hatred. Some lessons can be very simple and in this category I would sometimes put forgiving yourself, loving yourself more or being more patient with yourself. Others can take a lifetime. They all come to us when we are ready to receive them.

Here's a variation on this exercise: Write down everything that is not working in your life. If possible, write several pages. Next, quickly scan what you've written to see if certain words show up frequently. Let's say the word 'control stood' out and was used more than a few times. Then ask yourself this: "Am I controlling? How or who do I try to control? Am I afraid to let go of someone or something? What is my control about?" Keep asking questions and write things down as they come into your head. Get out of your way and let things flow.

When I did this exercise the word "control" kept popping up. I knew I had an issue with control, I just was not sure how controlling I was or even why. Doing this exercise made me sit up and take notice of my control issues. I had to be the centre of attention and I had to control people and the conversation.

I use to give big parties and loved having 40 or 50 people in my small house. Everything had to be perfect. Guests would arrive and I would spend all evening running from one room to another, spending just a few seconds with each of my guests. I had to make sure everyone was having a great time and I would be exhausted at the end of it all. But I was certainly in control and I was definitely the centre of attention. Once I realized that I wasn't actually enjoying these events, I stopped having big parties. Now I invite just a few friends over and have a much more enjoyable time.

Each day is an opportunity to learn about life and about ourselves and to notice what is being served to us on that silver platter; we have to be living consciously. I find it interesting that people will go to school to learn about a new subject or perhaps how to build something yet we are not as keen to learn new things about ourselves. Many of us fear change. Some of us would rather things stay the same.

It's important that we know that stasis is okay, too – you do not need to take the path of self-development now. It might not be the right time for you to do that, and your learning could be to just honor where you are today in your life, and forget the rest. Just keep reading and see this book as a story. One day something will click inside of you and then your gates to your mind and heart will be open to receiving all this new information.

Recap

If you are ready to want to make changes in your life you need to take action. Start by getting very serious with yourself. Ask yourself questions. That's right, start taking to yourself and LISTEN to what is coming back at you. I talk to myself all the time. We have great conversations with me, myself and I. Listen and learn, for within you lives your truth.

There are a few exercises that I've mentioned which requires a bit of writing. You can either do this on a computer or by writing it out. I had found that writing it by hand was more powerful for me.

Sometimes I would be blocked and forget what I was writing about or I would go around in circles. It was suggested that when this would happen I should change hands. So if I wrote with my right hand I would put the pen in my left hand. I was a bit weird when I did this. My writing would be all wonky and sometimes unreadable.

Supposedly this process got me out of my way so I stopped analyzing everything I was writing and it was my inner child speaking to me. Hey whatever worked and I wanted all this writing to help me get out of my rut.

There were times I wrote when I got very angry and towards the end of pages of writing the anger dissipated. Other times I would write when I was sad and the tears would roll down my face and soak the pages as I wrote. At the end of the all I did feel better and most of the times I did help myself to resolve whatever ever needed to be healed. The answers where right in front of me.

> "The level of thinking that got you to where you are now will not get you to where you dream of being."
> ~ *Albert Einstein*

11 Pinch me – I am alive!

Are you consciously living your life or are you on standing on a platform with the rest of the world, waiting for the train to pick you up and take you somewhere else? Did you notice the brilliance of the sun as is rose in the sky this morning? Too much smog, maybe you should move! Did you look up and see all those fluffy clouds, aimlessly floating along? What did you notice? What did you miss?

Did you pull yourself out of bed, drag yourself to the bathroom and then try to decide what to wear as you dreaded another day of work? Did you sit in your car, stuck in traffic, knowing you were going to be late? Or were you on a bus, swaying with the motion, jerking forward as the bus came to a stop and more people squished on. What did you notice? What did you miss?

Let's say it's evening now and you are at home, grateful for that. You get your dinner and sit your fanny in front of the TV, listening to all that terrible news about people who lost their homes or jobs or lives. Then you go to bed and get real revved up because you get to do the whole thing again, tomorrow?

At what point do you shake your head and wonder, "What is real?" There were times where I had to pinch myself just to make sure that I was awake because some times I could not believe what I was seeing or hearing.

When you start choosing to live consciously, you will see how much power the media has. The sad thing, it is mostly a negative power. People are afraid of hypnosis yet they will turn on some sort of media and fall into its trance.

To a large extent, our media dictate how to look, how to behave and what you need to do to succeed. You must be perfect looking, with perfect hair, teeth, figure, clothes. You have to drive the perfect car, live in the perfect house, with the perfect spouse and perfect job.

How many of you compare yourself to what you see on TV? Based on what you see or hear through the media, how many of you think we are not good enough? You may not be consciously aware of the discrepancy but your subconscious mind knows!

Look at the movies that promote violence. There are movies that are teaching hatred and making it seem acceptable to judge someone because of their skin colour, religion and/or beliefs. What do you think these movies are teaching you and our children? It's scary to think of how many people go see these movies!

I could go on about how the entertainment media affects the economy, how drug companies control our well-being and how the news media has carte blanch to say, do and show whatever they deem appropriate for their viewers.

Why am I bringing this up and what does it have to do with living consciously? Living unconsciously you get sucked into the void where the reality created by others becomes the standard by which you measure your own life. You find fault in yourself and in your neighbours. You are stuck on the platform waiting for a train that isn't even going to your desired destination.

We need to take the time to enjoy the wonders of this planet! We need to watch the sun set or rise, notice a stranger's smile or hear a friend's kind words. Have you ever gone for a walk in the pouring rain and felt the raindrops rolling down your cheeks?

Living consciously lets us see all the gifts that are presented daily. We can see the sun that brings warmth and love into our world, or rain that brings in new life. We can hear the birds singing to us and enjoy crickets lulling us to sleep. There are many joys handed to us daily and you'd be amazed at how many more you can discover once you start looking for them!

You begin to see life as it is, as a gift. Perhaps you are sitting on a bus or train feeling low and notice someone smiling at you. You're not really sure why – are they flirting with you, or are they actually focusing on the person sitting behind you? You wonder why anyone would ever smile at you, especially a stranger?

One evening, I went walking with my neighbour. I said, "Hello," or "Good evening," to each person we passed. After a while my neighbour said, "Gee Christine, you are a very friendly person and so kind to perfect strangers." As I pointed out to her, a little kindness goes a long way. I told her of a time when, feeling low, I had decided to go for a walk.

I was lost in my self-pity when a person walked towards me with a big smile on their face and, as they passed me, they wished me well. This lifted my spirits enormously! A perfect stranger had reminded me that I am not alone and that, really, all I had to do was open my eyes and become aware of my surroundings to find a little joy I had not even believed existed. That smile made a huge difference in my life and now whenever I pass anyone, I say "hello," or "have a good day."

When we live unconsciously we generally react without thinking and it's like we are walking around in a daze. If someone says something unkind to us, we respond with a sharp, unkind remark. If someone yells at us, we yell back, maybe even louder. If someone hits us, we hit back. It's a vicious circle and one way to stop all this madness is to focus on living in the Now, on being wide awake, with our feet on the ground.

They say the youngest in a family is usually spoiled rotten. I was the youngest of five and I was by no means spoiled. I was ignored, sent to my room, blamed for things that I did not do, ordered around – in short, I was subject to the usual verbal and physical abuse that most families accept as part of normal life. There was no love thing going on in my childhood!

Because I didn't know any other way of life – and nor did my family members -- I thought it was my duty to put up with abuse and allow people to say whatever they wanted to say to me: I was the youngest and that's just the way it was supposed to be – I thought.

In some ways, it was almost as though I gave my siblings permission to say or do whatever they wanted to me. And they sure knew what buttons to push to make me react like a raving lunatic!

It wasn't until I was in my 40's that I began to understand that I had to retrain people to behave appropriately around me. It took a lot of courage, persistence and strength to do this. I realized I had a choice: I could either move to another part of the world where I could start my life over or stop what was going on in my own backyard.

"Everything begins and ends with you." I've said this many times throughout my life and throughout this book. It has been a powerful reminder to me of where my responsibility begins and ends.

In order to change how people treated me I needed to begin with myself. I needed to start treating myself with respect and love. And I had to live consciously, awake and aware. Otherwise I would fall back into my old ways, my unconscious ways, treating myself poorly and allowing others to do the same.

I remember having a conversation with one of my sisters that absolutely pushed me to my limit. I had reached my boiling point and told her that the way she was speaking to me was unacceptable and if she couldn't speak kindly to me, we were finished. I couldn't believe what she said next: "But we're family!"

And I thought, "What, I'm supposed to put up with your verbal abuse just because we share some parents? Is there a special "Family" rule book somewhere that says I must abide by your abuse?"

When you live consciously you create your own rules and choose what is acceptable and what is not. *You start to treat people the way you want to be treated.* Your senses come alive, seeing, feeling and hearing things for the first time. It's almost as though everything is anew, like a baby opening its eyes and seeing for the first time. This is where you need to begin, from the beginning, as though you are opening your eyes for the very first time. Allow yourself to be like a baby full of curiosity.

Make *conscious* choices. Start to use your 'Free Will'. If one choice does not feel right, then make another choice, always honoring yourself, your neighbor and the planet.

Living consciously, you will start to hear your very strong inner voice speaking to you, a voice that may be barely audible at first because you've spent years letting the static in your head drown it out. When you live consciously, you begin the process of connecting to everything around you and within you, and you'll feel your inner strength growing, followed by a peaceful feeling washing over you. When I first started to feel this I began to say to myself, Welcome home! And then the goose bumps would run up my arms.

You might also begin to hear and/or feel your spirits gently nudging you, doing their best to guide you. Some people are uncomfortable with the idea of spirit entities connecting with us here on Earth and that's fine with me. Whether you want them or not, they are there waiting patiently for your questions. They are your life-line to your Source, guiding you, protecting you, and keeping you safe.

When you are confused and not sure what to do, just close your eyes and ask the question you seek the answer for and listen to what you hear. The first few times you do this you might not hear a thing because you head chatter is too loud or maybe you just doubt in this process.

Times I would go to bed in confusion and as I tossed and turned I would finally settle down and started to ask for guidance. I would slow down my breathing and calm the voices in my head and listen and wait. Sometimes in the morning I would wake up knowing exacting what to do.

Your own power plant.

One thing I can tell you is that once you feel that inner peace, once you know it exists, you will always try to reconnect to it. Like a pigeon thrown out into the universe, it knows where home is and will always find its way, no matter what. Your home is where your heart lives in peace and harmony.

But there are bound to be days when you're off balance, where nothing seems to work and you feel the world is out to get you: how can you stay connected to that inner peace? Do you have to escape to a mountain and sit there for days and say "OM"? Do you need to hide in a closet to escape from people and their madness? Would meditating for 10 or 20 minutes help you reconnect to your inner power? The answer is that they will all help, but some solutions will be more appropriate and efficient than others.

I'm sure you know the kind of day I'm referring to -- where you feel totally zapped, like a car that has run out of gas. Running home to make dinner or even lifting a finger to wash your own face, is almost beyond you. At the end of the day, your energy is gone and all you want to do is find a couch and stay there until morning tracks you down again. How can you keep the tank at least half full and the car running on all cylinders so you feel zippy again? That's a very good question.

Let me illustrate the answer with the following explanation: The electricity in our province is produced by a company called Hydro Quebec. It has major power plants which supply electricity throughout the province and the excess is sold to other provinces, states and businesses. When the weather gets too cold or too hot, demand for power rises, and this can potentially overtax the system and a major power failure might result. If that were to happen, the system is shut down and repaired and when ready, it comes back on line. Presto, we have power once again.

Now, see yourself as having your own personal power plant, your own built in Hydro Power. Each morning you get up, *consciously*, with your batteries recharged. You are in control of your thoughts and feelings and choose how you want to spend your energy. You see co-workers fighting and instead of judging them or putting your nose where it does not belong, you send them love and hold compassion for them. A client is angry with you and feels you let them down or that you screwed up. You know you did the best you could for them and realize their anger is not directed at you; you decide not to make the problem personal and instead of fighting back you ask them what you could do to make it right for them.

Living consciously helps you to step off the other person's treadmill of anger or other negative emotion. It keeps you grounded and lets you act from compassion, rather than keeping you stuck in reacting to whatever they are dishing out. The end result is that you maintain your energy, and can stay balanced with a level head.

When you live unconsciously, you are stuck in a reactionary mode. Your energy ends up being scattered between your bouts of anger and frustration -- you might end up yelling at people and any thought or feeling you have that is negative ends up zapping your energy. At the end of the day, you are exhausted!

Do you want more energy at the end of the day? Then start controlling your own power plant by living consciously, choosing to act from a place of love and compassion. Do you like to feel exhausted and worn out by end of day? If so, live unconsciously, react to situations in a negative way and continue to engage in the chaos of the world around you. That will do it!

Over time and after many self-taught life lesson, you will begin to realize that anger directed at you is not always about you. When you live consciously, you are able to distinguish between what you need to take responsibility for and what belongs to others. Why did you react before? Because you were living unconsciously. Now you know it's not always about you, it could be just that other people are struggling with their own problems and issues and you simply triggered something in them because you were in their space, so to speak.

Everything happening to you and involving you is there to teach you something. Remember my silver tray? You can ignore all those life lessons that are presented to you every day but the price is that you could be missing out on something special!

What do you think you would learn from adding fire to someone else's already glowing argument? A simple thing like walking away – and *not* reacting or getting caught up in someone else's drama – could be all it takes to keep your Power Plant running smoothly.

It would be very smart of you not to say or do anything that could either make the situation worse or make another person feel worse. You now have the inner strength to hold compassion for others and let go of any judgment, which means you do not criticize, make a comment or throw your two cents into the crowded disagreement. This is the power of being conscious. This is where your power is, in consciousness. Is it always easy to do? Of course not! It's much easier to write about it!

When you react to any negative situation, you give your power away. Going back to my Hydro Quebec image: there is only enough power to cover a certain area. Tax the system and you end up with power outages. Tax your system and at the end of the day, you are zapped, depleted, done in and maybe very ill.

Recap:

How do you keep all your power, so at the end of the day you feel calm and in control, instead of crazy and out of control? You can't do it if you live unconsciously. NOW! NOW! NOW! You need to be awake, aware and conscious, making sound choices instead of chaotic ones -- or worse, being a major contributor to the chaos. It does not matter who is at fault -- someone needs to be the adult and it might as well be you!

Living consciously, discovering who you are, becoming your best friend, peeling away the anger, fear and hatred, will only bring you joy, peace and happiness. You are on a journey of self-discovery. The more you find out about yourself, the easier it will be to act instead of react.

When you live in the moment you are in control of everything, including your thoughts. You begin to make your own choices, throwing away what does not work for you and surrounding yourself with what does. You hold on to your Power Plant and at the end of the day you will feel more at peace with yourself and with those around you.

I've said this so many times throughout this book, "This is your life's journey and it is a one step process". This is not about how big of a step you can make in one day, it is really about noticing all the little ones, because those are the ones that add up to being enormous. Any change you want to make takes a commitment and a promise to yourself that you're worth it! Aren't you!

"There is a giant asleep within everyone.
When the giant awakens, miracles happen"
~ *Frederick Faust*

12   It's okay to love yourself!

When I was growing up, I never understood the meaning of love. My parents had their tender moments, yet they were few and far between. I was not surrounded by physical love, although we had a lot of things. Image was important to my parents. We lived in a middle income area, and I was expected to dress the part, behave, curtsy, and speak when spoken to. When I was bad, which seemed often, it was no TV, or to my room!

I grew up feeling confused about many things. When I was in grade school, the bus stop was at Rosemary's house. Her mother was a very kind woman and when it was cold or raining she would pile us all into her home to keep us warm until the school bus arrived. Rosemary came from a family of seven kids and everyday her mum would hug each one of her kids and tell them she loved them and she hoped they would have a good day.

I came from a family of five kids and no-one ever hugged me, told me they loved me or wished I would have a good day. As a matter of fact, no one hugged anybody in our family and the words "I love you" were never said. And therein lay the seed of my confusion: why did Rosemary and her brothers and sisters have love and I did not? Was I bad? Did I have to do something special to earn it? Maybe I was too ugly to be loved or simply not good enough?

When I got older I went out to find this elusive love, which was a journey that involved a string of one-night stands. I was out to prove I was worthy of *something* and I went for the best looking men I could fine. I had to prove to myself that I was not ugly after all, despite my brother's constant criticisms of my looks growing up. He had some pretty interesting names for me – like sea hag and dog face – and they had left a mark.

I became a real estate agent and one day a man walked into my office wanting to buy a house. After I sold him one, one thing led to another and I ended up moving in with him. All went well for a few months and I decided they were going well enough that I thought it would be a good idea to get married. I popped the question, he said yes and off we went.

At the time I truly did think I loved him, even though I did not really know what love was. Whatever I had felt at the time was a new emotion for me and I just assumed it was love. Oh, wrong again. Infatuation will often masquerade as love and that must have been the state I was in because it didn't take long before I started finding big holes in the marriage.

This was an interesting situation to be in. I was very confused about my marriage and how I felt about my husband; I was extremely confused about my own behaviour and even wondered if I had any feelings at all. I felt numb, feeling almost nothing at all.

I was a Catholic so when I got married the commitment was to stay together until death; asking for a divorce was not something I wanted to do. I knew I was unhappy and I knew I needed out of the marriage. My spouse was quite happy and very confused about why I was suddenly so unhappy.

At first I blamed him for all of my unhappiness. Then I blamed him some more. I moved from being an unhappy camper to a very angry, nasty B....h! The angrier I got, the meaner I became. My world was breaking apart and taking me down.

The whole marital experience was very painful for both my husband and me. After all was said and done, I promised myself I would never cause so much pain to another human being for as long as I lived. And I knew I needed to figure this all out or all my relationships would be nightmares. My marriage was one of the first and most significant events where, thank God, I woke up to realize there was so much more I needed to know. I had to figure it all out if I wanted to lead a happy, joyful life.

I wanted to know and understand everything about love. I started to read books about love and became even more confused. The books made love sound complicated – or was it just me? How could that be possible? So many people around me said they loved someone. Were they lying or were they confused too?

At the same time, the media always showed images of people loving other people. Was this a farce or was I missing something? I was getting more and more confused yet determined not to give up on understanding all the things about love I just didn't get. I kept reading, attending courses and trying to understand.

When I heard someone say to me, "The only place you will find love is within yourself," I am sure I had him repeat himself because this blew my mind. What did he mean I had to love myself? This was a rather new concept. I think I sat there with a stunned look on my face with this thought just rolling over and over in my mind.

My Catholic upbringing had completely neglected the idea of anyone loving themselves. As a matter of fact it was a no-no. You were supposed to Love God first and then love everyone else second. I had a hard time with this concept, especially when it came from the Church. It seemed odd to me that priests would tell members of the congregation how poor they were and then expect us all to give more at collection. It was hard to square that off with the appearance of bronze 'No Parking' signs in front of the Church. There were days when it was 100 degrees inside the church and women – good Catholics all of them – would keep their fur coats on for the entire service. There seemed to be a lot of hypocrisy involved in this concept of love.

But loving yourself was never a part of the sermon and at age nine it was confusing to be told that we needed to love our neighbours, give more money to the church because they needed better 'No Parking signs' and love God. As a child I wondered, how it could be possible to love someone you couldn't see and I didn't understand why I should love strangers. It just seemed bizarre and complicated, and it left a mark.

When I began my new journey, my goal was to keep things as simple for myself as possible because anything complicated might throw me off track. In a way it would give me an excuse to go back to my old ways. But strange as it may sound, the biggest and most important lesson for me to learn was the simplest one: I had to learn to love myself. It took me a few years to figure out how to do this and it sounded far too simple – but it was an extremely important step.

When I was a Life Coach, I always ask my clients what one thing they could do for themselves that would probably change the way they look at their life. Most of them sit and look bewildered and wait for me to proceed with a long and complex explanation of some complicated issue. My response is always simply, "Love yourself."

If they looked bewildered at first it isn't long before they start to look scared and overwhelmed. Some say, "Well that sounds easy." Others just sit waiting for me to ask another question – which is always, "Do you love yourself?" Eyes pop out, fear grows on faces, concern and dismay rules. People often appear to be embarrassed by the question and typically I will hear "maybe, not all the time," or just plain "No."

Finally I would ask my client what they could say or do for themselves to help them love themselves? Once again, a state of fear seems to arrive out of nowhere. Some might look up at the ceiling, some will become teary-eyed, some look even more bewildered and others simply say, "I don't know."

The lesson becomes easier if I turn the question around and ask, "If someone you know were sad, what would you say or do to help them feel better?" The answers flow easily at that point -- I would give them a hug, tell them they were okay, tell them I loved them or do something kind.

"Very good," I say. "So what could you do for yourself to show that you love yourself?" Confusion arises again, and this time I will ask, "What did you just say you would do for someone who was sad? Could you not do the same thing for yourself?"

I also add to the list: Be kind to yourself. Stop putting yourself down! Speak kindly to yourself. Give yourself a hug. Take a break. Do something nice for yourself.

It amazes me still that this is so hard for people to understand – I can only surmise that we've been brainwashed into believing that making changes within ourselves is a monumental task and requires years of therapy. Nonsense! Just do one thing differently and the rest will follow!

Stretching for love

I felt really lucky because whenever I got stuck in my stuff a teacher showed up with some guidance or insight. As they all pointed out the key part to any learning, is about being kind and loving to myself.

I was really having a hard time understanding the concept of loving myself. Having graduated from the school of hard knocks and passing with honours, loving myself was definitely a foreign language. I was a Master of putting myself down and did it better than anyone else because I had studied and practiced it well.

The teacher I was working with asked me to stand up. He said, "Imagine yourself standing beside you. Stretch your arm out, palm facing downwards and rest it on top of your imaginary head. Start saying all those nice things you say to yourself." I was not sure what he meant because I never said nice things to myself. So he helped me with the first one and then I took over with ease: How can I be so stupid? I am such an idiot. Am I dumb or what? I am so useless I will never get this. I am the dumbest of them all and I will never amount to anything.

As I got into it, he said, "Each time you say something nasty about yourself, lower your hand." So I kept going until I was bent over and my hand was about a foot off the floor. Then he asked me, "Who do you think is underneath your hand?" I was about to stand up when he said, "Don't move." He asked me again. "Who do you think is underneath your hand?" Looking puzzled I said I did not know.

He said, "Remember when we started this process, I asked you to imagine yourself standing beside you. Each time you said something bad about yourself you lowered your hand. Each time you lowered your hand you were actually squashing yourself, pushing yourself down into the ground. Your hand is resting on the head of the imaginary you. Knowing this now, how do you feel?" I said nothing, but I shuddered.

I thought I was a victim because people always seemed to be unkind to me. Actually, I made myself a victim, blaming others, pointing fingers and beating myself up. I began to see why I found myself alone a lot. If I could not like myself, why or how could I expect others to like me? Maybe if I started to treat myself with a little kindness, then other people might do the same.

But I wondered how I could change years of negative programming? How could I change the negative voices in my head? I was full of questions and I wanted answers, now! Being very impatient with myself, I found myself becoming easily discouraged and frustrated.

It seemed no one had simple answers or easy solutions. Everything seemed to be a challenge with roadblocks on every corner. There were times I believed that I had a few screws loose because I could not understand nor grasp what I was reading or hearing. Yet, I was determined to get this, no matter what!

My first task at hand, "How difficult would it be to start saying nice things to myself?" Was it something I could do in a day? Did I have to memorize things or write things down? How do I go about this?

Presto, another teacher appeared and had few more suggestions. "Christine, you need to set an intention of how you want to be with yourself, a year from now. Create a movie in your mind, see what you need to see, feel what you need to feel and hear what you need to hear. Centre all of it around being loving and kind to yourself. You also need to make a deal with yourself to treat yourself with love and respect. Write things down that are important to you.

"If you wanted to help a sad person, what would you say or do for them to help them to be happy? See yourself helping that person and remember that you are actually the sad person you are helping – you know how to do this."

In the beginning, this was very hard for me. Just trying to find kind words for myself was like speaking a foreign language and the whole process sent shivers up my spine. But I managed to pick a phrase that was simple and easy to say. After a couple of days I started to sound like a parrot, "I love myself. I love myself. I love myself." Did I feel anything? Was this working for me? Each repetition felt more weird than the one before and sometimes I would just laugh and think how ridiculous this felt and sounded. This did not feel like progress – in fact, quite the reverse. I became discouraged and slipped back into being hard on myself. Then I felt like even more of a failure. This was certainly not easy! Eventually I got back on track again.

There were days where I was pretty good to me and there were days where I failed miserably. Over time, after many challenges, my life seemed to lighten up slightly. I picked up the habit of apologizing to myself each time I put myself down. Eventually I noticed I was apologizing less and less often and now I never need to.

The exercise of squashing myself into the ground showed that each time I said something mean about myself I was actually hurting me and destroying my spirit. When my teacher first said this to me I reacted negatively and I pretended to not hear. Wisely, my teacher did not repeat the statement, perhaps knowing that one day I would react in a more positive fashion. The problem was that my Catholic upbringing meant that anything associated with God or Spirit repelled me.

Over time I learned to love myself and it was this first step that gave me permission to accept me for who I am. When you can love yourself, totally, without wishing you were shorter; taller; skinnier; fatter; lived in a better home; made more money; or any other criticism you can think up, the world around you will reflect that love back to you in a positive way. Everything begins and ends with you!

We were placed on this Earth filled with pure love. Somewhere along the line we lost our way. Someone once told me that we are all Unique Pieces of Divinity and that we mustn't forget it!" Well I did forget and sometimes still do and I've been known to drive around with a sign on the dashboard of my car that reads, "You are a Unique Piece of Divinity" just to help me remember what I so easily forget.

The media has done a fine job showing us how not to find love. We've been lured into believing that buying things guarantees happiness and that love is in there somewhere. A television commercial selling diamonds says, "Show her how much you love her by buying her this beautiful 5-karat diamond!"

So if he can't afford the pricey diamond does it mean he doesn't love you? Another typical ad shows an attractive man or woman driving a sleek sports car with an attractive passenger by their side. Does this mean you need to have a sleek car to find love? Do you get nothing without it? Commercials are confusing and I guess the hope is that you will confuse love and happiness with purchasing power. It just doesn't work that way.

Another step closer to love?

Here is another amazing teacher story. When I got onto the trick of "loving myself" and wanted to understand it better, I put a message out to the universe and what showed up? You guessed it, another teacher. He told me to go home, look in the mirror and tell myself that I loved myself. I thought this was a very funny thing to do and I laughed – an old nervous habit. I remember thinking, "This will be a walk in the park." It sounded simple enough and since I was looking for easy things to do, I said sure, sounds great and off I went, giggling.

When I got home I went into my bathroom, turned on the light and stared right into the mirror. I kept staring and staring and nothing would come out of my mouth. The words were there, right on the tip of my tongue. But would they come out? No!

Then I took a long hard look at me it felt like I was looking at a total stranger. As a matter of fact it felt a little creepy. From that point on, I felt uneasy anytime I needed to comb my hair or to put on some makeup (thank goodness, I did not wear a lot of makeup!)

Before this little exercise, I never really focused on me when I looked in a mirror. I had been simply and unconsciously doing whatever I needed to do to my face or hair, and just wanted to make sure that everything I could see was in the right place.

After about a month or so, I decided to give it another shot. Do you think I could look into my eyes and say I love me? Nope! This simple little task was challenging me and it was beginning to drive me nuts.

I thought that if I got used to saying 'I love me' that might be half the battle. I just started saying, "I love me. I love me." I spat the words out of my mouth, like hot peppers. I repeated the words until I began to feel it in my body. What did that feel like for me? When I said, 'I love me' I felt goose bumps all over and my hair stood up on the back of my neck.

I can't remember how long it took before I could look in the mirror and say "I love me". This probably sounds very silly to you and at the time it did to me. Yet I went from sweaty hands, to how stupid is this, to goose bumps running all over my body and finally really feeling it in my heart. Was it worth it? You bet! Was it easy to do and did I change overnight? Of course not! But when I had completed this assignment I realized that another piece of the puzzle had just clicked into place.

More love stories.

We rarely think of the impact withholding permission to love ourselves has but here's a story that might help you understand how important this permission is for our selves, our spirits, our soul, our joy and our happiness.

Imagine you want to adopt a three-or-four-year-old child that an adoption agency says has been verbally and physically abused its entire life. You feel very sorry for this child and proceed with the adoption -- but little do you know how much time, patience and love it will take to help this child begin to feel safe.

Each day you show the child how much you love her by hugging her, playing with her and speaking kindly to her. There are many times you want to give up, may times where you had to bite your tongue from saying the wrong thing yet you remembered the commitment you made to yourself and to this child. As time passes, a friendship blossoms, which is built on trust and love.

This child you adopted and healed is in actual fact the child that lives within you. He or she is a part of you that has been squashed, shoved into a corner and ignored. Knowing this now, how committed are you to your own cause? What is your first step? What action are you going to take to help this child in you to heal? How much time are you willing to put into undoing the years of programming in your head? What is it worth to you?

Recap:

This is about learning to love yourself. Start by giving yourself the permission to go there. This is really not all the complicated. Just start saying nice things to yourself and be kind and good to yourself. Go for a walk when you need some space. Say "sorry" to yourself when you put yourself down. Look in the mirror and smile at yourself. Give praise to yourself. Pat yourself on the back when you did a good job. When you screw up, remind yourself you are doing the best you can with what you know. Talk to yourself the way you would talk to your best friend.

I am so relived we have hands free cell phones. Now when someone passes me by and sees my lips moving, they will probably think I am talking to someone on the phone. Little do they know.

Just for a minute, if you could imagine that everyone on this planet bought my book and took the time to learn to love themselves? Oh, I would be very rich! Kidding aside, can you begin to image how much better life would be for all of us, if everyone loved themselves? No wars, no hatred, no anger. Just a bunch of people getting along like one big happy family – we'd all be helpful and not looking for a return favour. What a concept!

News Flash!: you can't change the world – you can only change yourself. Live by setting an example!

> Your vision will become clear only when you
> look into your heart. Who looks outside, dreams.
> Who looks inside, awakens.
> *~ Carl Jung*

13 How grateful are you?

I have a friend named Peter, who was not a very happy camper. He complained about his job, which he hated. He complained about his parents, who fed and sheltered him whilst he cleared up his debt so that he could move out and find his own place. He also was unhappy because he could not find a mate. As a matter of fact, Peter had a very dismal outlook on his life.

It was not all doom and gloom because when he spoke of the things that excited him, he lit up like a Christmas tree. So, I knew underneath all that negative crap, lived a man wanting to come out to find a more positive look at his life, especially after hanging around me for a few months.

On our road to building a friendship, Peter found it interesting that I was always seemed to be upbeat about things. One day he asked me, "How do you manage to be so happy, always so cheerful no matter what shows up on your plate? I responded by saying, "A good portion of my life was filled with anger, hatred and sorrow. My life was full of chaos and pain. When I started this new journey of self-discovery, my goal was to live with joy and happiness. This was a commitment I made to myself, for myself."

Peter responded by saying, "It takes time for a massive ocean liner to change direction. It can't stop in an instant or turn on a dime nor can people do the same with the way they think or feel, can they?"

"Is that a statement or a question?" I asked

"Both!" Peter replied.

I thought about what he had said.

"What a brilliant analogy – and such a thought-provoking question from someone who was so negative!" I said, "Wow Peter, essentially, this is a great way to look at how simple or how hard it is to change direction in life."

I went on to note that navigating through choppy waters is like being in control and taking responsibility for our lives. It can take a lot longer if you do not have a proper map or compass and the process won't be as smooth and efficient if someone else is at the helm who doesn't know exactly where you want to go.

But every good sea captain knows that no matter how choppy or rough the waters are, eventually calmer seas will prevail.

Like an ocean liner trying to change direction we certainly do need time and patience to change course in our world and the only place to begin is within ourselves. In Peter's case, the first thing I suggested he do to change his own course was to start being grateful for everything he has in his life, even if it is not exactly the way he wants it. When you become grateful for what you have, then your life seems to lighten up a bit and things or situations might not feel like such a burden.

Peter was not crazy about his job and he hated going to work. I pointed out that his job might not be his "choice" job, it paid the bills, got him out of debt and brought him back some freedom.

Peter felt a lot of guilt over having moved back into his parents' home and he needed to let go of this negative feeling. He had a huge debt to pay off yet he felt he was far too old to once again rely on his parents. I told Peter to get over it! Although his father did not think moving home was the best move for Peter to make and he was not about to make his son's life at home comfortable and cozy. That being said, I am sure he did respect what his son had to do. I suggested to Peter that instead of finding fault in his parents' behaviour, he needed to be simply grateful that they were in a position where they could take him in.

"Just think if they could not take you in, were would you be?" I said. "In bigger debt?"

Peter needed to step back and stop feeling like a big failure and start looking at his life from a place of gratitude. He needed to be grateful for all that he had, his health, his ability to think and breathe. He also needed to be grateful for the food he ate, the water he drank, the beauty around him, the sun that rises and sets. For his friends, for the people he's known, for guidance when he needed it, for the body he was living in, for being alive. The list is endless.

He needed to stop finding fault in everyone and everything; I told Peter that looking for what was positive and good in his life would make it show up more often. Being grateful is an important step. I warned Peter that all the negative thoughts and doubts he had about himself, his life and his job were sure to keep yanking him off course.

I am sure you know someone who complains all the time. They complain about the weather, their spouse, their job, their dog, cat, you name it, they will complain about it. They complain about what someone should have said or done for them. They complain about someone winning something. When you think about it, some people can come up with some pretty interesting things to complain about.

Nobody likes being around these people! If you are a complainer, might I suggest you stop? People will distance themselves from you, if they haven't already. Really work hard to finding goodness in everything! Over time, you will make your burdens feel lighter.

Peter found that seeing only negative things about his parents made his situation more unbearable. Once he switched the way he was thinking and became more grateful to them for letting him live under their roof, things became more bearable for him.

At the time I was writing this book my mum was 91 years old and still living on her own. She neither could see nor hear yet managed rather well. There are those odd days where my mum would slip into being a negative nanny (as in goat) and I guess at her age she was allowed. I would gently remind her that she was neither bedridden nor stuck to a machine to help her breathe. She could walk on her own two feet, were many her age couldn't. I would also ask her what she could be grateful for. She didn't exactly love it whenever I would remind her of these blessings but what's a daughter for?

With a bit of coaching she generally began to rattle off a few things and once she got the hang it, the good news just poured out of her. For a few minutes, she had a smile on her face and forgot about the things that bugged her about being alive at the age of 91.

Some more magic!

There are times when I am in a rush and need to get from point A to point B very quickly and safely. In my way is a gauntlet of roadwork, traffic and lots of traffic lights. Before I get into my car I will say to myself, "I need to get to point B as quickly as possible, so I need all the lights to be green." Inevitability, all the lights would be green and I would make it to point B without breaking any traffic laws. Once I am at my destination I say "Thank you for getting me here, safely and on time." This does not take a lot of thought or effort to being thankful.

Here is a real simple one, "Be grateful for the food you are about to eat." Here is what you can say, "Thank you for this food I am about to eat." You can say it out loud, say it to yourself, cup your hands over the food as you say it, or not.

Each night before I fall to sleep I go through a ritual. I thank God for all that he has given me, for another day to play, for the people that have come into my life, for situations that I learn and grow from, for the food I eat, the water, air and sun. I thank Gaya, goddess of the Earth for her beauty, for keeping me grounded. I thank my Guides, Angels and Masters for their guidance, love and wisdom. Then I send my love and gratitude to everyone and everything that exists.

This takes all of about two minutes. By the way, if God is not part of your belief system, pick your Source, your Creator, whomever you believe to be your Higher Source.

Each morning before I get out of bed I take the time to meditate (any where between five and thirty minutes) and set an intention to how I see my day playing out. I am grateful, once again, for another day to play, to learn and grow. I see myself smiling, being happy, honouring, loving, respecting and trusting everyone and everything that shows up, and most importantly loving myself. I start and end my day by being grateful.

What are you grateful for? Go ahead and grab a pen and write down at least 20 things you are grateful for. It might give you a different perspective on your life. It might also help you to begin focusing on what you have rather than what you don't have.

"Just imagine that the purpose of life is your happiness only – then life becomes a cruel and senseless thing. You have to embrace what the wisdom of humanity, your intellect and your heart tell you: that the meaning of life is to serve the force that sent you into the world. Then life becomes a joy."
~ *Leo Tolstoy*

14 A movie in the making!

Imagine yourself being the director of a major film production. The movie you are about to produce is "Your Life!" A director needs a good script to follow or the movie may end up on the floor. It can take months, if not years, to complete a good script. As the cast of characters play out their parts, the editing continues. It is a lengthy process yet in the end the movie is a success. Here is how you could make your movie a box office hit

When I started my career as real estate agent in the late 70's I was making between $35,000 - $45,000. At the age of 27 I was happily prodding along, making what I thought was a decent income.

Then I decided to change companies so I could live closer to where I wanted to work. Within a few months my new boss saw potential in me and told me that I could easily earn $100,000. To me, that was a lot of money and the sound of it scared me. He said that if I wanted to make that kind of money I would need to set some goals. Not knowing what he meant I listened to him and put into action what he told me. I began plotting out my future for my career to making lots of money.

At the beginning of each year I sat down and wrote out how much money I wanted to earn. Then I figured out exactly how many buyers and sellers it would take for me to make that kind of money. I broke everything down from a year to months to weeks to days.

I got very excited about the whole concept because that was a decent chunk of change. It did not matter if I believed I could do it, my boss did and that worked for me. Maybe he was right, all I needed was to believe that I could.

The first year I set the goals I was off by $10,000, which was pretty cool. The following year I made exactly what I set out to do and kept it up for ten years. In the beginning it was fun setting goals, checking each month to make sure I was on track. If I was off, then I worked a tad harder the next month.

After about seven years something inside of me changed and I was not sure what it was. Setting goals became an unpleasant task and it had become more of a challenge. As the year came to a close I knew I needed to write new goals for the following year. It felt like I had to start all over again, which in actual fact I was doing yet it felt like an unpleasant chore.

I stopped looking forward to the New Year. Goal setting was worse then having my teeth pulled, with no anaesthetic. I got harder on myself and then fear set in and the dialogue started in my head, "What if I do not make these goals, what will people think?" My mind was working overtime and I was no longer having fun. Money became my enemy and after being very successful, I left the business. I was literally unhappy making money.

When I heard the word 'goal' it made me cringe. As much as goals helped me be successful, they also stressed me out. I had to keep up with what I wrote down because to me, it was carved in stone, even though I knew it wasn't. Also it was very important to be better than anyone else. The constant dialogue in my head kept me awake at night, "What would people think if I did not reach my target? They will see me as a failure. They might not like me anyone."

The other thing I hated about setting goals was now I had to be accountable. And if things did not materialize the way I wanted, then I was only confirming how big a failure I was. Can you just imagine what it was like growing up in my head? Those thoughts had high class sneakers on, running havoc and driving me nuts.

After leaving real estate I started taking different courses to hopefully light up my path so that I could figure out what to do with the rest of my life. Over the years there were courses that I took which included other ways to setting goals. Since I was no longer goal-driven I looked at this new information from a different perspective and created a new platform for creating goals/desires.

One of many steps

I needed to change the way I looked at goals but I also needed to drop the word itself from my vocabulary because it no longer excited me. The concept had to relate to my future, the life I wanted to live, rather than the sterile setting and achieving of objectives. I realized I was my own tour guide on this journey and that I needed to become more creative in plotting my course. I had to keep my desired destination in mind. "Goals" had to become about creating a map of where I was and where I wanted to go. Now how exciting is that? I began to plan how I wanted things to be. I am my own film director, creator and designer. I am the Captain of my own ship navigating the world. The sky's the limit!

You can do this too -- think about what gets you *excited*, what words move you? Use them to make this process as *real* as possible. You need to *feel* what you want to *feel, see* what you need to *see*, and *hear* what you need to *hear*. Use all your senses to give your journey *meaning*, to give it *life* and use your imagination to do it. Your thoughts are a guiding system that helps you set your course. Plug your desires into your thoughts and fire the whole system with some emotional energy that simulates how it feels to get what you want and presto, you've created your dream life!

Is this something you can whip up in a few minutes? That depends on how important it is to you -- so it can take some time. Something that worked well for me was to write my dream life out one day and then a day or two later go back and reread what I wrote. Sometimes I would change a few elements, other times I would add some new ideas in or take some features out. I got in the habit of tweaking my vision until it suited me perfectly.

One *big thing* I didn't realize in the beginning is that what you are writing is *not carved in stone*. These words can be changed around, erased, scratched out or torn up – you always have choices. You are the one and only one, who is in control of your life. This is your destiny!

Here are a few ideas that might help you plot the course of your journey:

When writing your goals, be specific and use short, clear, simple sentences. Do not use words such as 'and' or 'therefore'. Never use negative words: there is no place for "don't," "can't," "won't," "no," "'but,'" or "try."

This example is not the best: *"I want to be able to own and run my own company selling widgets (positive) and I don't want to work 24 hours a day (negative)."* A positive with a negative gives you a negative. Basic math.

This example is *dry* and specific enough to could work: *"I own my company. I sell widgets. I work as long as I need to work"*.

This example is a little more exciting using more energetic words which will help in the manifesting process: *"I am the proud owner of this amazing company, with a dynamic team selling products that are in great demand. I love what I do and it brings me a lot joy knowing I am helping many people."*

This is *your* script of *your* life. Make it meaningful to you but don't include other people in the hopes they will follow your cue and don't write goals for your children or anyone else you care about because that doesn't work. You have no control over other people's behaviors or outcomes -- you can only control your own space, your own life. This is *your* journey.

This might have been my downfall initially because while my goals were directed at making plenty of money I was focusing on impressing others rather than sustaining myself.

Write everything as though it is happening right *now*. Keep it in the present tense. Your mind does not know the difference between, past, present or future. Writing in present tense can make it happen faster. Pretend it has already happened. You are tricking your mind into believing that you already have it.

Example: *"I am now earning $$$ per month. I am in a loving relationship. I am married. I am sitting on the beach.*

Avoid using words in the future tense, like "I will," "soon," or "next." Focus solely on what you want and erase all thoughts of what you don't want.

Example: *Say "I am successful" instead of "I don't want to fail", "I am happy" instead of "I don't want to feel sad", "I am a non-smoker" instead of I want to quit."*

Be honest with yourself and make your goals realistic. If you are selling widgets and in five years you want to be a brain surgeon, you need to ask yourself if this is realistic.

I've helped numerous people set up their vision framework over the years and when they were done working on their part of the project they would send it back to me for feedback. Many people had trouble with the idea of "realistic". I don't use the word to hold people back from shooting for the stars, but rather to keep things in perspective and most importantly, achievable. Otherwise it's easy to become discouraged and give up.

Generally speaking, people who were not realistic about their vision for the future were typically people who truly believed they were failures and that they would not amount to much in the world. By setting very lofty goals they would set themselves up for failure and this would reconfirm for them how stupid they were. This would then give them permission to beat themselves up even more and the cycle would continue. Avoid that trap!

You need to breathe life into your words. Get excited! How does it feel having accomplished what you set out to do? What do you hear, see and feel having done so? As I mentioned before, use all your senses. Make your words jump off the page. If you're dry or flat with your words, then your life will be dry and flat.

Pay attention to the words you use to define how you feel. When I ask someone how they feel having accomplished a goal I typically hear "I feel fine" or "Great," or "It's okay." How can these words get anyone excited about their life?

This is where your imagination needs to come into play. See, feel and hear whatever it is you want.

Example: Lets say you want a partner. You need to see this person in your life -- what does he/she look like? What does it feel like being in their arms? What do you hear them saying to you? Bring those feelings and the pictures you have in my mind and breath them into your vision of what you want. – and trick you mind into believing this person is in your life now.

Example: You want your life to be filled with peace. What does it feel like to have inner peace? Do you feel it when you are in the country or walking along a beach? Take that feeling of peace and breathe it into your life.

Example: Lets say you want rain because it has been very dry. Imagine your feet playing in the mud that was made by the rain. See everything around becoming wet. Hear the rain as it hits the window. Feel it running down you face, wetting your hair, the clothes you are wearing. Experience these feelings in your imagination and breathe them into your vision of what you want.

Be specific. When do you want your goal to happen? What month and year? Give yourself a time frame.

Example: If in five years you want your own company, pick a month, day and year that you want this to happen. Then determine what action you will take between then and now to make this happen. Write down everything you think you need to do to make this company become your reality. Maybe you need to take a few courses on accounting, learn some people skills or create a web page.

Chunk everything down so that it does not feel overwhelming to you. Plot out when you need to do things over the five years. If you need to take some courses, sign up for them. If you don't your plan is just a bunch of words on a page.

TAKE ACTION! This is probably the piece most people neglect. I've seen many people write up pages of what they would like to see happen in their life and never take any action. It's like they think it will just land in their laps. When it doesn't they say, "What a waste of time writing out what you want!" People can be so funny sometimes!

Taking Action requires movement. So this means, you need to do something physical.
- You want to lose weight and you decided you are going to walk every other day. So walk!
- You need to take a course to help you earn more money or maybe change careers. Sign up for the course!
- You are not happy with your relationship and you want to change. So get guidance or leave!
- You hate your job and really should spend the time to rewrite your resume and get it out there. So, do it!
- Are you just a lip service? All talk and no Action? If you want something to happen *you* need to take Action!

Whatever it is that you want, you need to get OFF your butt and do it!

Describe how will you know you've achieved your goals. If you are planning a trip, how will you know you are there? Are you holding the ticket in your hand or do you see yourself sitting on the plane?

You want to start your own company -- how do you know you've done it? Do you see yourself walking in the front door with your company name overhead? What do you feel being your own boss, having people working for you? What do you see happening around you? What are you saying to yourself? What are others saying? What do you know now, that you did not know before?

You want a new car? Do you see yourself sitting in it or driving around in it? What color is it, the make and model? What do you see as you drive this car. What do you feel like sitting in this new car? What does this new car feel like? What are you saying to yourself as you are diving this car? What do you know having this car? You need to give your dream 'Life'. The words need to jump off the page.

Since we grow and evolve daily, yes daily, our desires and dreams will do the same. It is important that you revisit what you've written, daily. It is like planting a seed, it needs a bit of water daily, or otherwise it will not grow.

The neat thing about this whole process is that when you write things down you become a participant in your own life. You become excited about it and the endless possibilities it contains. Your life seems to come alive as you breathe fresh ideas into it. You feel more in control and your life feels more like an adventure. You're always looking ahead and every time you turn a corner you are met with a wonderful surprise.

Another big mistake I made in my early goal-setting years was to omit balance. Everything I did was solely about my career and because I never really focused on any other part of my life, I was living out of balance. It was like trying to walk a straight line while holding a few bricks in one hand. After a while you might drop the bricks or fall over, which is what I did with my real estate career, my marriage and I am sure a few other things

I wondered how to create balance. Again, different courses taught me that six areas are important in life and when you begin to create your future, you need to do it in each of these areas: Career, Relationships, Family, Spirituality, Health & Fitness and Personal Growth.

It's a good idea to rank them in terms of their importance to you, and start with the most important one – it will usually take the longest to do. As you proceed to the ones that follow, the whole process becomes easier because you are more focused and you realize this is not as complicated as you might have thought.

Steps to creating your dream life

Below is a chart that you could use to help you stay on course. You might look at this as a purchase order because you are making a request. If you were a company and wanted to place an order for office supplies, you would need to be very clear with what you were ordering or you might end up with the wrong size of paper or not enough of another product.

This also applies when you are creating your dream life. You are making a list of what you desire or else you might end up manifesting something you did not want.

Take the form and photocopy it six times, one copy for each area you want to work on. If you have any long-term goals you might need to produce a few more copies to cover one, three and five-year time frames. Find a quiet room, turn off the phone and maybe put on some calming music.

The trick here is to just begin. This is not a race so take however long you need. Maybe your first step is to Take Action! Shall we begin?

Creating your dream life:

Today's date _____ Completed date _____
(5,3,1,YEARS OR 6 MONTHS FROM NOW)

FOCUS: Career – Relationships – Family – Spirituality - Health & Fitness - Personal growth. Pick one.

1. WHAT DO YOU WANT? Own a company? Lose weight ? New job? Find a mate? Buy a car? Join a fitness club? Go on a trip?

2. WHAT DOES IT LOOK LIKE, SOUND LIKE, FEEL LIKE? (Describe this in detail) You need to see this in your mind as though you are watching a movie. Example: If you wanted a new car what would it look like, sound like and feel like. The car you want is a sports car – what kind is it, what color, shape and size? Is the interior leather or cloth, what color? Does the engine purr? When you sit in the car what does it feel like? Do the seats mold your body? Is the leather soft? I think you get the idea of Step 2.

3. WHAT DO YOU FEEL HAVING THIS?
What emotions are present? How do you feel looking at this car sitting in your driveway? How do you feel as you sit in the drives seat? Now you are driving down the road, what are you saying to yourself, what are you feeling?

In Step 2 you are describing what you want. In Step 3 you are breathing life into it. You are giving it color, making it exciting. Whatever you write the words MUST jump off the page. This is a key component. If you can not get excited about what you want, then don't expect the universe to respond.

Another way to look at these steps: Step 2 is what you created in your brain and Step 3 is the elevator going down to your heart. Whatever you wrote in Step 2, allow it to settle in your heart and now say how it feels having what you desire.

Want to lose weight? How do you see yourself having lost the weight? What are you saying to yourself, how does it make you feel? Please do not say good! Use exciting words. Words that motivate you.

4. WHAT STEPS (ACTION) ARE YOU PREPARED TO TAKE TO MAKE THIS HAPPEN?
You need to take physical ACTION. If you want a new career then go job hunting, redo your resume. If you want a better job then maybe you need to take some courses. Enrol in some classes. TAKE ACTION! Otherwise, all your hard work, all you have written, will just die on the page, along with your dreams.

5. HOW WILL YOU KNOW YOU HAVE THIS?
What will you see, feel, hear and know once you have whatever it is that you want in your life? If you wanted to go on holiday, do you see yourself sitting on the plane or do you feel the sand between your toes as you walk along the beach? If you want to open up your own company, do you see your name over the door?

6. REPLAY IT AGAIN AND AGAIN
Take a couple of words or phrases that help you to reconnect with what you've written. Let's say you want a new mate in your life and hugs are very important to you. See and feel this person arms around you. Here what they might be whispering in your ear.

Each time you bring this picture into your mind, surrounded with all the feelings that you feel in your body, you are giving the picture more power. That power creates a vibration (remember every thought carries a vibration), which is sent out into the universe. Hence helping you the manifest what it is that you desire.

7 BE THANKFUL! BE GRATEFUL!
This only takes a few seconds to say Thank you. Thank you for my life, for the food I eat, for the beautiful loving people in my life, for my health and the health of my family.

15 Are we done yet?

Do you remember life as kid going through grade school? I remember being taught the importance of being better than anyone else and how you got there really did not matter. My goal was to get as many gold stars by my name by the end of every week. At the end of the month the one with the most gold stars won a prize. Guess what, no matter how hard I tried clawing myself to the top I never did win a prize. That should have told me something!

Going to school was all about learning and at the end of the year, if you studied and did the work, you passed. If you did not do the work, you failed. Most of the subjects we had to study were never really all that important, were they?

There were basic lessons at home that we acquired a long the way: how to make the bed, clean the bathroom, wash the dishes, do our homework, what to do and what to say…If you did not do what you where told there were consequences. For me it usually meant no TV, no phone calls with friends, or I was sent to my room. If that did not get my attention, then my parents would take away the thing I loved the most: I could not go to the stable to be with the horses. That got my attention. This was blackmail at an early age.

Life's Lessons = Wisdom

I might have fallen asleep or missed the class in school where they taught that learning equals wisdom. I did not know all of life's lessons you receive bring you closer to understanding who you are, helping you to form your values and the principals by which you live. What's this about wisdom? How much wisdom does one want and for what reason? I was quite happy just plodding along, minding my own business, thank you very much!

Do you ever feel there was a reason for something to happen or for something else to show up in your life – yet you push it away? It's almost as if sweeping the idea under the carpet makes the issue meaningless and likely to disappear. I knew, deep down inside that all these life lessons would amount to something. I was just was not sure when, where or how. I just kept sweeping everything under that carpet. There were many days I would trip over that lump in the carpet yet I still managed to ignore it by walking or jumping over it. One can do this one's entire life or stop to take note and possibly begin to make sense of that impressive and growing lump in the middle of the floor.

Learning = wisdom" is very basic and simple.

Some of my experiences might help explain more about life's self-learned lessons – they are the gold stars we earn from our different experiences. When I was very young I went to an outdoor hockey game to see my brother play. It was very cold, and for some reason I decided to stick my tongue on the metal part of the hockey net out on the ice. You can imagine my surprise when my tongue stuck to it! Writing about it sends shivers up my back! I am not sure how I pulled my tongue free but I do remember the pain I was in and the layers of skin I left on that post. Ouch!

After that little adventure, no-one came running up to me to ask if I found 'the wisdom'. But I did say to myself, "How stupid of me – what was I thinking?" One thing was certain: I was never going to stick my tongue on metal again, hot or cold. One might say that is intelligence, which is also wisdom: short and sweet and to the point.

As we move into our adult life, those lessons keep coming. Some days you can be sitting there enjoying the scenery, things feel calm and you feel pretty good. Then out of nowhere, you feel like you've been hit or sideswiped by an event beyond your control. Your calm world is now upside down. Another learning is coming at you like a bolt of lightening and all you want to do is duck, put your head in the sand or just hope it will all go away. The lump in the carpet keeps getting bigger!

When you do not want to pay attention, those lessons might just turn around and take a massive bite out of your life ... just to get you to pay attention! Going to school to get a passing grade so that you can make it out in the world is one type of learning. But in reality, there are no courses in school that can even begin to prepare you for your life's learning's -- and that's a shame!

No matter how you slice it, the most important lessons are those that have been presented to you on the silver patter, that I've spoken off before. Those are your life's lessons. They do not teach these in school! Sometimes you are not even sure if what you took away from an experience was the "right" learning, and you won't really know until it happens again. That is the test: how do you act or react when the same experience crops up again in your life? Whatever you do, you are learning!

What are Life's Lessons?

Let's say you like to speed when you think you can get away with it. Typically when you take off there always seems to be a policeman waiting for you around the corner. You've forgotten how much you've paid out and you just got notice that another ticket will lose your license.

How many tickets will it take before you to stop speeding? How many policemen will it take to save your life and the life of others? How much money do you need to lose before you feel the pinch? Or will it take losing your license before you wake up? Do you value your life and those of others or will speeding take control of you? The wisdom might be: Live longer. Respect yourself. Be happy. Be nice to the police, they are only trying to save your neck and uphold the law.

The funny part about people who know they deserve the ticket the police officer wants to give them is that they go through a war dance with the officer. They have many excuses for speeding and 99.9% of them are lies. The people who rant and rave the most put a lot of energy into finding a crafty way to avoid paying a ticket. They go to court and play the victim role and lie through their teeth and refuse to take responsibility.

Back in my teenage hay days of drinking and driving I once found myself a tad confused and going the wrong way on a one-way street. It was late at night, I had had a few drinks and I was young and invincible. I remember being polite and thanking the officer who stopped me for basically saving my rear end but really I was hoping he would not give me a ticket. That did not work so I went to plan 'B' and got angry with the policeman, not that it mattered to him because he still gave me a ticket. Then I exerted some energy for a few weeks of ranting and raving, snarling at any policeman that crossed my path. Finally, out of the blue a thought popped into my head, "Christine, what do you think could have happened to you if that policeman had not stopped you? Do you realize you were doing the wrong way on a busy street, late at night? Do you think you would be alive today?"

Let's look at another example: you are racing to get somewhere and someone cuts you off. Do you smile at them or hold your fist up or do some crazy hand signals? I remember getting cut off all the time and it used to really tick me off. On one occasion, while I was ranting and raving to someone (another teacher) about this unfair situation, she said to me "Christine could it be possible the person was cutting you off to slow you down? Or maybe they were just there to wake you up so you would drive consciously?" There is wisdom in all of this and the question is whether or not you want to see it or keep ranting and raving and playing the role of a victim in your life.

16 Living consciously?

A teacher once told me we receive between five and ten life lessons a day. I thought that was a big number and decided to find out for myself. Each night as I lay in bed I would think about my day and what I missed and what I got. To my surprise, some days there were plenty and other days there were none.

When you live unconsciously, living in robot time, your head in the sand, you'll miss everything. Then there will be times when you hit your elbow or knock your knee and do a big time ouch! This is how your guides and angels try to get you to wake you up to the 'Now' time. You might not realize there are amazing energies out there, doing their best to keep you living consciously. They have their gentle nudges and if that does not work, look out.

Being on this new journey of mine I had made a commitment to myself to really do my best to live consciously. To me this means being wide awake all the time and not falling into an unconscious mode of existence where you wake up every few hours and wonder what you've missed. You probably know what that's like – say you get into your car to drive to work and before you know it, you are sitting at your desk wondering how you got there. You've missed something

I can remember once driving in my car, vacantly minding my own business when somehow my tongue found its way between my teeth. Suddenly I chomped down very hard on my tongue and screamed 'ouch' about fifty times. It was extremely painful. In a split second, I went from anger to laughter because I realized my guides must have tried nicely many times to encourage me to live consciously. But I must not have been paying attention to those little nudges they had been giving me and a good chomp on the tongue brought me back to earth.

Five a day?

At some point I realized the importance of getting my "learnings" – my life lessons. I figured the more "learnings" I would get the faster I would evolve and get through wherever I was to get to wherever I needed to go. It almost became a race to me. For whatever reason I felt that there was a time limit on everything. The need to know and wanting to understand everything, was vital and I had to get it Now!

This is not always how things work as the universe works on its own schedule. There were many nights I would lie awake playing back my day looking for at least five lessons. Once I found what I thought was a learning, then I would play it out in my head, madly searching for the wisdom that was connected to the learning.

When I messed something up, when something did not feel right to me, where I felt out of control or close to it, I knew this was a situation that had a learning for me. I desperately looked for the wisdom because I knew if I did not get it, it would keep coming back to taunt me and this I did not want. I felt compelled to figure it all out, all at once.

All though this I was doing a very good job driving myself crazy. If patience was to be one of my lessons, I guess I was not getting it. I am sure you can guess where me stress level was.

Then a Teacher appeared and I told him how effective I was at driving myself crazy. He laughed and I laughed but I still wanted the learning so I could get the wisdom that awaited me. My teacher laughed a little more and he told me to stop seeking. I looked at him, perplexed. I closed my eyes and tried not to cry tears of frustration: "What do you mean, stop?!"

My teacher went on to say that the learning would come when the time was right. "You don't need to focus on learning, all the time. Just let things go Christine, and the wisdom will come in time. And stop driving yourself crazy!" Easy for someone else to say!

My Understanding

The way I see it, a "learning" is a lesson there to teach us about ourselves: maybe how to be more compassionate, accepting, giving, forgiving and holding unconditional love for ourselves and others. Learning will show us what we can do or can not do and what we need to change within ourselves.

I've learned other things about this "learning stuff," too: like a scratch in a record, the same song can play over and over again until we are awake enough to change the record by changing the event, by changing how we behave or by changing what we say or do. If not they will follow us around where we keep finding ourselves in the same situation – the details might be different, but the story is still the same.

As you go through life you will notice similar learning showing up, learning what you thought you had forgotten. Yet is it a test to see if you really got the learning before. They want to see if you behave differently. For me it was a benchmark because I would think back on how I would have once behaved and realized how much I had grown because I did not react. No buttons for anyone to push because they were gone

I had mentioned before about a client who lived through two abusive relationships. For years she blamed and hated both of her husbands. After I helped her find the positive aspect of those marriages she was able to find the wisdom she was meant to gain from those experiences. Her anger and hatred for her ex-spouses dissolved as she finally realized she was worth much more than she had originally thought.

My client's new found wisdom taught her the importance of loving herself. It taught her to hold compassion for her ex-partners because they were doing they best they could based on what they knew at that time. Since my client got the lessons she needed from those pivotal events, she knew she passed the tests the universe had presented her and felt she would never find herself in another abusive relationship. She was able to move forward through her life with having a better opinion of men.

Learning is not all complicated. Most lessons are rather simple yet sometimes very hard to cope with. Especially when it is connected to someone you care about. Below are a few more examples of lessons that many of us need to get.

You are rude and mean to people. You never have anything nice to say and all you do is yell at everyone. People try to tell you to stop yelling and stop being so mean. Are you listening? Then you noticed that when you walked into a room, people walked away. What do you think your lesson could be?

How about being grumpy? I call them the negative nannies (as in goats) of the world. You complain about everything under the sun. Nothing works, its everyone's fault and the sun did not rise on time! You say that no one likes you and you have no friends. Go figure! What possibly could be your learning?

The more you learn the easier and lighter your journey becomes because you are not towing around all that negative stuff. Your life will change, your friends will change and always for the better.

Life's lessons are there to help us evolve. That is if you want to evolve. You might be very content you your own world, thinking everything is rosy, and that is fine. If you do not want to learn it today, trust me it will keep showing up. If you don't get it now maybe you might get it in another lifetime. Believed it or not!

> "Living consciously involves being genuine; it involves listening and responding to others honestly and openly; it involves being in the moment."
> ~ *Sidney Poitier*

17 How do you measure up?

I've attended many different kinds of "schools" in my life and another real favourite for a time was the school of Judgment. With a lot of hard work and dedication, I passed with honours. I just loved judging people, because at some level I figured I was a perfect specimen of a human being. It did not matter how people talked, walked, dressed, lived or breathed, when they came into my view I judged them from head to toe.

I could be eating in a restaurant, strolling in a mall or sitting on a park bench, everything provided a front row seat for me and all that was missing was the popcorn. I was terrible. Looking back, I still shake my head. Knowing what I know now, I realize how unhappy and fearful I was back then. Who made me Queen for the day?

We are living in a society where judgment is the norm. In corridors and offices and around the cooler, you can hear people dragging others through the mud, and all because they might not think the same, speak or dress the same, or even look the same. Differences are seen as wrong.

We also have measuring sticks for comparing ourselves to others, and most of these measuring sticks climb up into the clouds and out of our reach – they are about perfection. It's no wonder we beat ourselves up and then easily turn around hurting others with our words and actions: we are frustrated with a set of unattainable goals.

Where do these measuring sticks come from? Why do we set them so high, out of reach? I think that our society has conditioned us into believing we are not worthy or good enough. Look at the programs we watch or the ads we listen to. We compare ourselves to what we see on TV or in print. And what are we exposed to? Messages about what we should wear, how slender and fit we should look, what possessions we need, how we ought to live…how can anyone possibly keep up with it all?

It's inevitable that we subconsciously compare ourselves to what we see and hear and once we realize we will never catch up to the ideal we find solace in judging others. The harder you try the further away the unattainable goals seem to slide and then somewhere along the line we see more desirable stuff and we subconsciously raise the bar, that invisible measuring stick, again. This is why it is so easy for us to beat ourselves up: because the bar we can't reach gives us permission, to find fault in ourselves and everyone else that crosses our path. They don't measure up so it's OK if we don't measure up. It becomes a vicious circle!

The measuring sticks we carry around hold all our frustrations of not being able to compete with others or never being good enough. These frustrations create a whirlpool of anger and fear. Remembering how emotions carry a vibration that can affect the world, now add more whirlpools of 'not good enough' along with the emotions attached to that, and what do end up with? A very unhappy and sick planet. What would happen if you did not have measuring stick?

Drop your measuring stick and you will start to find happiness that lives within you. Your frustrations will dissolve, your stress level will go down and all because you figured out that you no longer need to measure up to anyone or anything.

When I use to feel I had to measure up to someone or something I would ask myself, "Who raised my bar? Why am I doing this?" I would take a step back and realize I was creating new stress and frustration in my life. What a silly thing to do. I did figure out that the only competition I have, if any, is with myself.

My goal is to figure out how to be a better human being. What is your goal?

18 What is Judgment?

It is always interesting to see how one thing is connected to another and another and it goes on and on. All these links linking together are making a very long, solid chain. When you break one link then the chain breaks and it might take sometime before it gets reconnected or it may never get reconnected. Breaking one link in your chain could change how you see yourself and the world.

For me I feel that judgment was one of those major links in my chain. It is connected to your self-esteem and it's related to that invisible measuring stick that tells you about your inadequacies. It's about the chatter in your head that says you will not amount to much. It is the constant uphill battle with those demons you keep in your closet -- the failed diets, the failed relationships, the size 6 skirt you keep holding onto despite the fact that you are now a size 12.

It's also about the voices you listen to, that tell you what other people might be thinking or saying about you and driving you to second guess yourself to the point of destroying any possibility of winning against any odds. *Next time you find yourself there, I want you to say, "Says who?"*

Look into a mirror. Who do you see? That is who you are really judging. So now is the time to break that link in your chain.

What has helped me to stop from judging myself – and by extension, other people – lies in totally *loving* yourself. When you love, honour and respect yourself, there is no room for judgment to breathe. This means accepting yourself 100%. Stop thinking you are too fat or too skinny, too tall or too short, not smart enough to be a brain surgeon or capable enough to be president of a major company. Just pinch yourself and know that you are perfect just the way you are and you can be whomever you want to aspire to.

When a judgmental thought jumps into your mind and tries to seduce you into behaving the way you used to behave, remember that you are stronger now and shake those thoughts out of your head. Speak kindly and treat yourself with respect – that is your new norm.

When you find yourself in a group of people who are in judgment mode, you now refuse to become a participant. Instead try to nudge them into a more productive, kinder conversation. If that doesn't work, tell them you can't stand hear and listen to this kind of a conversation. Either they change what they are talking about or you will leave.

This is not an easy cycle to break because it is culturally-ingrained behaviour. It is broadly accepted behaviour that needs to stop. As I've said, the world can only change one person at a time beginning with each one of us. When someone judges someone else, they probably don't think to highly about themselves.

All the tiny steps forward will eventually add up to a giant step for you and this is what we need to keep reminding ourselves about. We need to set the example as to what is acceptable and what is not acceptable. If you stand there and add your two cents, then you are saying their behaviour is okay.

Judgment was also destroying my spirit, fogging up my vision and turning me into very unpleasant company. Mind you the company that I use to keep quite enjoyed my two cents.

As you take these small steps towards a happier life, know there will be days when things go wrong. You might fall back into your old patterns and judgment could raise its ugly head. You might catch yourself before you embrace it or you might not. And you know what? That's okay. We're not perfect! I always say that I am a work in progress and I'm doing the best I can! I also know that I am doing much better than I was a month ago, a year ago and ten years ago.

19 Who is taking care of you?

In the old days, men grew up believing their sole purpose in life was to get a good education, find a stable job, get married, have children and put a roof over everybody's heads. They were discouraged from showing any fear and they felt obliged to be strong always and not talk about their feelings. They could never get caught crying.

Women, on the other hand, were raised to believe their main purpose was to get married, have children, keep the house clean, cook and entertain. A mother's needs were put on the back burner because everyone and everything else was far more important.

Things have changed since then! Many women, married or single, cannot afford to stay at home to raise their kids. They hold down one if not two jobs and run from work to day care to the grocery store, to the kitchen table for homework supervision, to the stove to prepare meals and then back into the car to drive kids to hockey practice and/or ballet. Somewhere in there the house has to get cleaned and the bills must be paid. You name it they're doing it and they are exhausted, sometimes feel unappreciated and realize it is expected of them.

Women have been programmed into believing it is their responsibility to take care of others. It wouldn't matter how busy they were, everyone else's needs are met before theirs. At the end of the day they are flat out exhausted. As they lay their head on the pillow they wonder where the day went and make a promise that tomorrow they will take a breather and do something for themselves. Promises! Promises!

The next thing that happens is that stress levels rise, along with resentment. The person doing all the running around begins to feel like a robot. They feel no one really cares about them. Too tired to talk, it's common for communication to break down. We are all looking for affirmation – at some point one spouse or the other may be tempted to reach out to find someone who appreciates them more. Then the marriage falls apart.

It doesn't matter who you are, if at the end of the day you are at your wit's end feeling as though no one really cares about you or what you are doing, you need to stop the madness because it will destroy what you've been trying to keep together, namely your family. Since most of my clients are women, many complain about just that, how they feel and how they are being treated.

My response to them is, "What are you doing to take of yourself?" A wave of confusion usually reflects itself in their faces and they commonly say, "What do you mean, take care of myself? I don't have time for that!" If you do not take care of yourself, who will? If you do not take care of your own happiness, who will? If you are not happy with your life, how do you think the people around you feel, especially your children? How long are you going to pretend that everything is okay? If you don't stand up for yourself, what are you teaching your children?

As they sit and listen to me, fear and concern usually cover their faces. It's almost as though they stop breathing. Frequently I hear, "It sounds like you want me to become selfish?" In a sense, yes – but not to the extent of hurting or being cruel to another.

"How many people are trapped in their everyday habits: part numb, part frightened, part indifferent? To have a better life we must keep choosing how we are living."
Albert Einstein

20 Does selfish mean 'No'?

In the dictionary the word selfish is defined the way it is intended: *concerned with your own interests, needs, and wishes while ignoring those of others; showing that personal needs and wishes are thought to be more important than those of other people.*

Another word in the dictionary is self-interest, which is close to what I am propounding but still a little beside the point: *self-interest is the placing of your own needs or desires before those of others. I would like to add: so that you are happy and feel good about yourself and others understand that it's important.*

No matter what word you use, the goal here is for you to find some time for yourself, and that others respect your decision. You need a time out. You are responsible for your own needs, wants, desires and happiness. Start doing for yourself before you do for others.

A friend of mine who is a single mom, with two small children, explained to her children what she meant when she said, "Kids, mom needs some mummy time." Sue told them there are times when she needs to be by herself, to do things that she needs to do or just to take a break from it all and when she asked for this time alone, the kids respected this and gave her space. As the children played in one room, Sue was off in another room, doing her own thing.

There will be a word you will be using a lot if you want to start taking care of your well-being and that is "No!" It is not commonly used when saying it to someone you care about because remember, you've been programmed to turn on a dime! Another reason why it is not easy to say "No" to someone is because we want them to love us, we want to feel wanted and by saying no to someone, we might be tempted to feel they will stop loving us.

Take a minute and think about it, why do you do anything for anyone? Do you expect a payback, believing that if you do for them, then they must do for you? Will that get you into Heaven faster?

Think about a time when you wished you had said "No". What was the feeling or thought running through you? "If I say no, they might not forgive me. Maybe they will hate me and not talk to me anymore." Did it feel like you had guilt hanging around your neck? Then within a split second did you say "Yes"?

Here's the picture: You had a super crazy day, running from here back to there. You are at home and the kids don't get back from school for an hour. What joy, you get to put your feel up, relax, have a coffee, play some quiet music or meditate. The phone rings, it's your best friend or your mother wanting you to do something for them, and it must be done now! This means giving up that precious time you were going to use to recharge your batteries.

Here is a question you could ask yourself before you say yes or no, "Is what they are asking me to do a life or death situation for them?" If the answer is "No" then why not put them off? Guilt? This could be as simple as your daughter or son asking you to drive them somewhere. Now you say, "Nope, this is my time!"

Do you honestly believe they will disown you because you said 'No'? Do you really think they will love you less? The first time you say "No" they might well go into a war dance or pull a tantrum or two. They may say or do whatever worked successfully in the past to get you to help them out. If you do not respond the way they want you to, then be prepared for more drama! But please, sit down and enjoy the show or quietly walk out of the room. You need to stand your ground (in a loving way)! Don't you have a tantrum too – if you keep your focus and stay calm, they will get over it.

When you say no, mean it and don't waffle or others might see that tinny bit of doubt in you and easily coax you into a yes. The more they hear no, the more they will stop asking. You need to be consistent and remember why you are doing this.

Some people think if they push you hard enough, they will break you down and end up getting their way. Don't forget, you've trained them to behave this way. For years you've put up with their threats, slamming of doors, ranting and raving and that behaviour has worked! Sometimes you just gave in because you couldn't stand the noise any more or maybe you actually believed their threats.

What would happen if you said, "I can't do this now, I am exhausted or I am in the middle of doing something else which I must finish." If this person goes into a war dance, so be it! Hey they might even find someone else to do it for them or maybe they might even figure out how to do it themselves. It's a miracle!

Standing your ground!

Are you worth the right to take a break? If you don't think you are, then guess what -- you aren't! As long as you allow people to tug on you they will never disappear from your space. They are somewhat like a teacher, showing up until you decide to stop the madness. People are there to teach you about you and this includes your spouse, children, parents and siblings. How do you change the behaviour of other people? You can't! You can only change yourself!

Do you have any "negative nannies" in your life? They call you up at any time of day and keep you on the phone complaining about someone or something. I know you've got one or maybe three people like that in your life. You've given these people permission to behave this way and how long do you want that to continue? Just because you've seen the light and you want them to stop driving you nuts, please do not expect them to quickly stop a behaviour you've condoned for years! That won't happen, trust me! Been there done that and yep, another closet full of T-shirts to prove it! So chill out or you will wear yourself out – and them too!

Here's my story. My mum, who at the time was around 70 years old, was my number one negative nanny. I would be having a decent day and my mum would call me up and go into her stuff. She would complain about the family, the weather, her life you name it. Being the good daughter I was, I would listen to this and within minutes, my oh so fine day, has turned upside down and I had become the negative nanny.

I also had a friend who did the same thing, called to dump her stuff on me and again I put up with it. There were days where I felt really crummy because I had allowed these people to use me as their dumping ground. I gave them the permission to ruin my day.

On my new path of self-discovery I needed to take care of my space by clearing it all this negative nanny stuff out of it. I had to stop people from yelling at me, swearing at me, speaking to me unkindly and treating me with disrespect. I know now that they were treating me the way I was treating myself. I know I've said this many times, "The people you keep in your life are a reflection of who you are"! This can sometimes be a very scary picture!

We all have breaking points and one day I reached mine. I could no longer tolerate listening to people who constantly complained. On that day, my mum called and went into her usually stuff and after a minute or two of listening to her, this voice inside of me said, "Mum, you know I love you? Now, at the time I was not sure if I did or did not love my mum, but I had read somewhere that if you say you love someone it might help ease what you are about to say to them.

Anyway, I said "I cannot continue listening to you complain. Could you please change your tone of voice and maybe talk about something a little more joyful?" It was as though she did not hear me and continued with her tale of woe. Again I said, "Mum, I do love you yet I cannot continue to listen to you complain." I would switch to something more pleasant, and within a second mum was back into her stuff. Being firm, using a very calm voice I said, "Mum, if you continue speaking this way to me (now she was getting angry at me) I will hang up the phone and you can call me back when you have something more pleasant to say to me." I really did not think she heard me, because she still went on with her negative commentary. I might have had to say it three or four times before my mother said, "I am your mother how dare you suggest that you will hang up the phone on me!"

Those, "How dare you!" family rules kicked into place. It was a struggle for me to keep my tone of voice in check because my initial knee jerk reaction was to fight back, to get super angry and slam down the phone. Well this was the new me, or at least that was my intention. I kept my cool as my mother continued with more negative conversation, and then I took a deep breath and hung up the phone. Within minutes my phone was ringing off the hook. My sisters now were on the wavelength as my mother "how dared me" to death. Again those family rules kicked in, "That was your mother you hung up on, how dare you do that! How dare you speak to mother that way?!"

It did not matter how I felt. It did not matter that I told my mum I did not like what she was saying. Nope, none of that mattered. I should not have been so rude, should not have said, did or whatever, to my mother.

As I listened to them, a shiver ran through my body because I was realizing I did not matter to them. It was only important how they felt and that they were requiring me to respect them and the family rules – but not myself. As I bit my tongue, grasping the phone and wanting to smash it down, it became very clear to me, I was tired of being other people's doormat and continually giving people permission to wipe their dirty feet on me!

My mother did not speak to me for weeks which was drastic considering we used to speak at least once a day. She was a very stubborn person and in her mind I was being rude and arrogant. Then her dog died and she called me in distress. It was so very sad, my poor mum and Dad were devastated that their little Willy died.

From that point on, my mother knew I meant business and whenever she called and went back into to war dance about anything negative, she knew I would hang up the phone. Mum did her best to be positive around me but occasionally she would fall off track. All I had to do was say something simple like, "mom" and she knew.

My mum was doing the best she could with what she knew. How could my mum have known differently, herself coming from an abusive father and a mother who closed her eyes to it? Life would have been so much simpler if I could have walked into a library and found a book on "How parents are suppose to treat their children."

I would not give up on my principals for the sake of family. I knew I had to make a stand in a very gentle, loving way. I am thankful I did because the relationship I had with her is now built on love and respect.

This is not a one shot deal. This is something I had to do over and over again in a very loving way. If I cared about the person, then I used a lot of patience and gently reminded them how I've changed and pointed out what was important to me. People will only treat you the way you treat yourself. When you begin to realize your own importance, saying no is fine; Making your own choices is a good thing; Make time for yourself; put yourself first, be selfish. Otherwise you will always be last in line or someone else doormat!

Don't be afraid to give your best to what seemingly are small jobs.
Every time you conquer one it makes you that much stronger.
If you do the little jobs well, the big ones will tend to
take care of themselves.
~ *Dale Carnegie*

21 Relationships

You probably have read a few books about relationships. Typically they have titles like "How to build a good relationship with your spouse" and it's tempting to think this section of my book is similar. It is and it isn't. What all of those relationship books leave out of their considerations is the importance of "You"!

Have you ever felt inadequate because you were not in a relationship? I used to think I was a big loser because I wasn't involved with someone. Watching TV gently reminded me of my deficiencies. The ads all promoted items I should definitely buy because they would lead me directly to love with a tall, dark, handsome man who had a chiselled face, deep dark eyes, blond hair that flowed in the wind and a smile that could stop you in your tracks. Well, those ads pulled me in and made me feel real small.

I went through a good portion of my life looking for the ideal mate. I had a perfect list of what I expected and wanted in a man: he had to have a very good income working at a super job, he had to drive an expensive car, live in a very nice house, dress well and he had to be drop dead gorgeous. It was also important he could carry on a good conversation and not be a couch potato.

When we see a display of affection, do we assume it is love? Many people think so. A couple I once knew would crawl all over each other kissing and hugging as they sat in restaurants, walking in the park or watching movies. Sometimes it was unbearable to the point of disgusting. Friends used to tell them to go rent a room! Guess what? Within a year of marrying they were divorced. What was the point of their display? Did they need to prove something to themselves or others? Was the public affection about insecurity?

This book is primarily about discovering who you are and you may wonder what this has to do with relationships. Let me ask you this, "If you do not have a good relationship with yourself, how on earth, would you expect to have a super relationship with anyone else? It's not possible!

It is not possible to have a loving relationship with anyone unless you have a loving relationship with yourself. I know you might have heard me when I said it the first time but did you really hear me? You can not love anyone if you do not love yourself. Oh for sure you can pretend. Some days may be fantastic but the bad ones are really atrocious, aren't they?

When you speak unkindly to yourself you will in turn speak unkindly to your partner. If you are into beating yourself up because you are not good enough, then guess who else you are beating up, either verbally or physically. You will do this to your partner, to your children and even your pets. Your behaviour could also extend into your workplace. Does this make you joyful company?

If you do not like what is going on with the relationships you are having with others, then you need to change the relationship you are having with yourself. If you don't like a friend you can change them for someone else but if you have not changed within yourself then the next friend will show up with the same behaviours of the one you just got rid of. The merry-go-round just keeps going.

What is a relationship?

The dictionary defines a relationship as *the connection between two or more people or groups and their involvement with each other, especially as regards how they behave and feel toward each other and communicate or cooperate.*

My definition of a relationship is: *A spiritual, physical, and emotional relationship you have with yourself that is loving and characterized by honour and respect for yourself **at all times**!*

Can you imagine growing up with these values? Do you think you would settle in a relationship for just anyone? Do you think you would allow yourself to be abused or to be the abuser? Would you sell yourself short, put up with crap or continue being a doormat for someone else? I know everything is a learning and I guess we need to experience what we've chosen to experience in order to appreciate what we now have. But maybe the lessons could be easier!

Do you understand the importance of building a relationship with yourself? I mean a *good* relationship – that is what this book is all about. The relationship you have with yourself is like the foundation for a joyful and fulfilling life. A house without a foundation may not hold up during heavy storms and, trust me, those storms will show up from time to time!

I was playing golf with someone recently, who told me he had finally stepped off his treadmill that he called life. He had tried hard to make two marriages work, yet they failed anyway and although he was still friends with his former spouses, he knew he needed to become friends with himself. After some self-discovery, he realized he was a good person and he liked who he was.

He also began to see that there were a lot of nice people around him and he wondered why they were not there before. I told him they probably where there, he was just so caught up with what was not working in his life that everything around him seemed to be broken as well.

The saying "Stop and smell the roses" applies to befriending yourself as well. You need to stop and take a good look at yourself. You need to be honest, with yourself. You need to ask yourself some serious questions or you will continue on your own treadmill. And you need to appreciate yourself for your good qualities.

Nice to finally meet you!

It's interesting to note that when you meet somebody new you become very curious about them. If you feel some positive chemistry with them then you might even ask them a lot of questions about their life, their likes and dislikes, the books they've read, movies they've seen, etc. You want to get to know them as quickly as possible.

Why not ask yourself those same questions? Start with what is important to you in a partner? Write down your thoughts and when you're finished, notice that whatever you've identified s exactly where you need to begin with yourself. If you say you want someone who is honest, then ask yourself, "How do I need to be honest with myself? Drop that invisible measuring stick and start recognizing that you are fine exactly the way you are. If you want to lose weight, then do something about it. Take action! If you want someone to be open and easy to talk to, then guess where you need to begin? In case you've forgotten, "With Yourself!"

The object here is to get to know yourself better so that you can have a loving relationship with your partner, your children, and members of your family. Write down the details of what you like and dislike, what's acceptable and not acceptable to you, know what your behavioural boundaries are and tell people when they have crossed the line.

Building a foundation based on love and respect for yourself will bring relationships into your life that will last a lifetime. When you can embrace yourself, be happy with who you are, then the relationships in your life will reflect the peace, joy and happiness you have within you, rather than a fairy tale that has no basis in reality.

22 Responsibility

Scenario 1: It is late at night and you are tired, finally on your way home from a very long, hard day. You see a light flashing on your dashboard and it's telling you that you are low on gas. You figure you are good for a few more miles so you continue on home. The next day you spring out of bed, dress and fly out the door. As you snake your way through the traffic that pesky light starts flashing again – you need gas and, again, you ignore the signal.

Halfway between your home and office your car dies. You turn the key and nothing happens. The car is dead. You start to curse the car, getting madder by the minute. You pick up your cell phone to call the office and the roadside assistance crew. Guess what, the phone isn't working either. The minutes turn into an hour and you are beside yourself as you stare at that pesky light that's still flashing on your dashboard.

Finally you get to your office and you're late for an extremely important meeting. You blame the traffic, you yell at your secretary and you're screaming inside your head. You might even say to yourself, "Why can't my day start off well? Why am I always dealing with this garbage? Why does everything fall apart? I am sure someone is out to get me!"

Think of how much energy you've wasted fuming at every one. All this could have been avoided if you had filled up your gas tank and recharged your cell phone. What will you do next time a light starts to flashing at you? Hopefully you will make a better choice and correct the situation as soon as it arises, so you won't feel like screaming at the world.

Scenario 2: You have an important presentation to give. All your documents are in order and you know the material inside out. The day of the presentation you arrive early to set up your wall charts and make sure every seat has the right documents.

Just as everyone starts to arrive the audio visual guy arrives, late, with your overhead projector. He quickly sets up and leaves as you begin. You dim the lights and turn on the overhead and it does not work. You aren't sure what the problem is yet you keep your cool and ask someone to turn on the lights. You pushing buttons, flip switches and try everything you can think of – but nothing happens. Now you begin to loose your cool and someone suggests you plug the machine in. Everyone has a good laugh, including you.

When the presentation is over and you are congratulated for a job well done, you still feel justified in calling the audio guy and blasting him for not plugging in the machine. All you really needed to do was to be grateful that your presentation went well and next time take the time to check and see that the machines are plugged in and working before the technical expert leaves the room.

Scenario 3: You've just finished doing your grocery shopping. You are loaded down with bags and the clerk suggests a car order. You are in a rush and decide to do it yourself. As you work your way to the car one of the bags breaks. This bag happens to hold the eggs and milk, which are now splattered across the pavement.

You are not sure whether to laugh or cry yet you decide to march back into the store, ranting and raving. You blame the clerk for giving you a defective bag. As you keep yelling, the poor guy can't say a word, because the customer is always right. What he would like to tell you is he did not make the bags nor purposely give you one that had a hole in it.

These three scenarios give you an idea of how we tend to pass our responsibilities on to others. They show how we are quick to blame, point fingers, rant and rave, scream and yell, often at people who are only trying to help. Our society has made this behaviour very acceptable and now we need to stop. Oh, by the way these are just more of life's lessons to grow by.

We are taught this from a very early age. Kids show up to school without their homework done with a bank of excuses ranging from "the dog ate it" to "I was too sick to do it." In between are the excuses that it got lost or stolen. It almost becomes a game with children to see who can come up with the craziest reason for not doing something. School is a breeding ground for lying. And while people do what they need to do in order to survive and compete in this world, it still does not make it right!

Where do you think kids learn how not to take responsibility? They watch you, the adult doing it and doing it well. Some adults even joke about with their friends, how they got away with it. Or they feel superior telling someone how they raked a clerk over the coals for giving them a grocery bag that was defective. Omitting that fact that they tried to carry to many things and put too much in one bag.

Every action causes a reaction. These reactions can create either a positive or negative outcome. Think about dropping a pebble in the water and then watching the ripples the action creates. Do you know where those ripples end? They always connect with other ripples to create bigger, more powerful ripples.

When you want to react in a negative way, think about how your actions also extend outward like ripples. How many people become affected by your reaction? Could your one reaction create a wave of negative upheaval?

The story of the Hundredth Monkey is an example of how one's action or reaction can create a rippling effect. Scientists spent years observing monkeys on an island in the 1950s and found that the monkeys liked sweet potatoes but did not like the taste of sand. One day a monkey dropped a potato into some water, washed it off and then began to eat it. Within a short period of time all the monkeys where washing their potatoes in the water. Eventually, scientists all over the world were suddenly witnessing monkeys washing their potatoes in water before eating them. The idea just caught on like magic.

When you give power to a thought, it travels far and wide, like the 100th Monkey or the Butterfly Effect. What many people do not realize, is that what you put out there eventually comes back to you in one way or another.

Responsibility begins a home and your home is within yourself. What is the point to blaming someone? Before you get your knickers into a knot why not take a deep breath and maybe give your head a little shake and see if you really need to blame anyone. There is a good possibility you are the cause of your own mishap.

You need to start explaining to your children the importance to taking responsibility for what they were suppose to do or not do and avoid taking the slippery slope to being dishonest.

> Whether or not you have children yourself, you are a parent to the
> next generation. If we can only stop thinking of children
> as individual property and think of them as the next generation,
> then we can realize we all have a role to play.
> ~Charlotte Davis Kasl, Finding Joy, 1994

23 Who to trust?

When I was a child, horseback riding was vitally important to me but the jumping aspect of the exercise scared me. Frequent falls were no problem, landing on my head was fine, and getting knocked out didn't phase me. But looking at those jumps, which were much bigger than me, was just intimidating. I did my best to avoid jumping but since it was my goal to teach riding I figured I had to master my fear.

I remember watching a movie about a girl who loved to ride and she feared those massive jumps as well. Her teacher told her to trust in herself and to imagine her heart going first and watching it jump each time with ease. The girl followed the suggestion and over time she found her confidence and jumped everything in sight. It was only a movie, though, and I had a hard time transferring the idea into my own life, primarily because I didn't understand what "letting your heart go first" really meant. I remember thinking, "How do you do that? How can I take my heart out and watch it jump the jumps? What would happen if I fell, would my heart be there to catch me or would I once again land on my head?"

Like most children, I had a vivid imagination so I tried creating a picture of my heart and watching it jump before I followed along. I did one jump this way for starters and it seemed to work reasonably well so I did another one. And then another. As I began to feel more sure of myself I began to tackle two in a row and then more. Eventually I was able to jump nine or ten at a time. Because I learned to trust myself, I became confident about jumping.

When we are young we tend to trust adults because "they know better", or at least we think this is a safe bet. As we get older, however, we need to learn how to make our own choices and it doesn't always come easily. I can't count how many times I've second-guessed myself! You may have done this too --- you deliberate for ages before finally making a decision about something and then BOOM! You get in your own way by doubting yourself, instead of trusting that you have made the right choice.

Why is trusting yourself so important? Looking at my childhood dream to become a competent jumper, if I had not trusted myself I wonder if I would have continued to ride? Making the decision to leave my career in real estate to go off to explore human behaviour meant I had to trust that it was the best choice for me. Many people thought I was crazy to make this choice. Choosing to divorce my husband also won me the disapproval of many people who thought it was not the right thing to do. In the end, I had to trust that these decisions were right for me.

Another level of trust many of us struggle with has to do with the spirit world. Along my path I've had many teachers tell me that I needed to trust that I was not alone, that spirits and guides are always around us. Whether we are naughty or nice, rich or poor, there are many spirits waiting for us to ask them for guidance and help.

God (or whoever you consider the source of your Divinity) did not put us on this planet to be in pain, to live in poverty, to hate, to steal or to kill; these are the choices we've made. God's gift to us was "Free Will" blanketed in total love. Many of us have given up our "Free Will" by allowing others to make all our decisions. So in essence, they have given their "Free Will" away. It almost like being a puppet on a string. Allowing others to pull you around.

Although it makes some people uncomfortable and doubtful there is something bigger than us out there in the world and to deny its existence is to struggle. People who close their minds to the possibility are like the slaves who built the pyramids, pulling huge pieces of stone behind them and barely moving forward.

I have friends who can see spirits around them as clearly as you or I see other human beings. This really annoys me because I would really like to see a spirit, despite my occasional doubtfulness. I once said this to a teacher and he laughed.

He said, "Christine, spirits are not just from the spirit world, they are present in everybody you connect with, all of us carry a message of some sort. Think of a time you were not happy and a stranger walked by and smiled -- that's a spirit. Or remember when you misplaced something you needed and you asked out loud for help, never really thinking anyone was actually listening? When the lost item showed up, that was a spirit at work."

I have super golf Spirits/Angels. They save a shot that was just about to go into the water. Miraculously the ball hits a rock and bounces back onto the fairway. Comments from the group, "You live well, Christine!" And I say, no that was my golf Angel.

Spirits come in all different shapes and sizes and when we can't actually see one we need to simply trust that they are there. We need to trust that we are not alone, that we are safe, protected and most importantly, always loved.

Many of my clients have told me they have at some point felt very alone. My response is always the same: "You need to know that you are not alone, trust that you are surrounded by spirits who are waiting for you to ask them questions. They will help you and guide you if you will only *Trust*!"

In the beginning this was a hard pill for me to swallow because I did not believe in a God. How could I be expected to Trust in myself, let alone in a non-existent God, and then move on to believing in spirits? So it was a challenge to work my way through all this new information.

Eventually I came around and started to look at my spirits in a different light. I also needed a new way to get myself quickly out of situations what would make me get angry with myself. I got into the habit of looking up to the heavens and saying, "Okay, you guys up there, I can see you are having a good laugh on my account and I also know that you've made a hefty profit by selling tickets so all your cronies could come and watch "Christine's hours of laughs".

Oh, by the way, when I get up there I expect a cut in the profits!" Humour has been my saving grace. Without it I have no doubt I would have been locked into a white jacket and stuck in a padded cell.

As I sit here writing I know I am not alone -- my spirits are here in my office. I can't see them yet I can feel them, a hand on my shoulder, goose bumps up my arm and then all these words fly across the paper. Is this me doing this all by myself or is there a 'them' out there too? I am sure it's a bit of both! We make a great team!

A friend of mine, who is also another teacher for me – taught me a humorous way of looking at life, and I've adopted her framework. It's helped me through some dark and dreary moments. The technique is to see a large number of spirits gathered around a very large dome looking down at the Earth, at me in particular, since they are my own guides. They have just spent a few days creating a new path for me to follow. They've picked out the people who are going to show up and help me. They're so excited to see their plan in motion because they know the outcome will be just perfect for me.

So there I am, walking blindly through this unknown plan, and for whatever reason I am trusting in something bigger than me. The guides are watching my progress and they're becoming increasingly pleased with themselves. Suddenly, I take a sharp turn off their planned path. Within seconds the heavens are filled with chaos as they scramble wildly in an effort to regroup AND to get me back on track.

They probably tried hard to grab my attention so I wouldn't veer off their perfect path but I was probably in an unconscious state at the time, totally ignoring them. In the course of the day in question, I had probably hit my head a few times, or knocked my knee and yet I still missed their jolting signals.

When I realized there was something out there much bigger than me, when I started to believe that I was not put on the planet to be miserable, when I started to grasp the meaning of trust, my life started to transform.

I can't stress this enough, *"Trust in yourself."* Trust you are not alone. Trust that you are being guided and loved, no matter what you say or do. Trust you are not being judged because it does not exist in the universe – judgment is a human trait!

Your past does not = your future

Some people believe that whatever happens to them in their past will follow them into their future, like a bad dream. In many cases, they're right. Other people think they need to go into their past lives in order to get at the source of their current problems. Some people come up with the craziest ideas on how to fix their past -- sometimes they choose the hardest route.

I remember, way back in the early 80's, I was curious about past lives because everyone was talking about it. Someone told me they knew a lady who did past live regressions and she was very good at it. I was in so much pain I thought this might help me straighten my life out. I called her up and made the appointment.

When I got to her home I was surprised as she met me at the door. I expected to see someone tall and skinny, scary with long stringy hair and a big nose. This lady looked quite and that concerned me. We sat down and she had me shuffle some cards, which I then placed in front of me. She asked me if I liked having things tight around my neck and I told her no.

She went on to say that in a past life I was hung because I was a witch. Relax, I was the good witch from the south or west. Then she asked me if I liked to swim and I said yes. Do you like to go under water for long periods of time? Well I guess as long as I can breathe. I had a past life where my foot got stuck on a branch that was under water and I could not get free and therefore I drowned.

These stories where fine and dandy and awfully interesting but I was not sure how knowing this could or would change my life. Did I care that I was hung from a tree because I had different beliefs or that I drowned because a tree would not let go of my foot?

We are funny creatures because we are always trying to find answers about ourselves, often in the wrong places. We go to a therapist who probably needs more help than we do. Or we sell all our belongings and go live in a commune because we want to escape from the world. We seek out a past life therapist because they're going to unlock all our deep dark secrets and we'll wake up a whole new person!

You are a collection of memories, and that is your history. Be it good or bad, it is who you are and you can not run away from it. Mind you, there are those who think if they change their job, spouse, or where they live, their life change for the better also. And it might improve for a while but the fundamental issues haven't changed, the life lessons haven't been realized and the story will pick up where it left off. You can run all you want but one day you have to wake up and realize you did not get far – everything is exactly as you left it.

You can rewrite your history to include and exclude whatever you want. You can continue to live the life of a victim or take back your power and live your life the way you intended it to be.

We are all individuals with individual needs, wants and desires. We either live our own dreams or continue to live someone else's. "Whose dream will you be living? Mine, yours or someone else's?" The choice is yours and it always has been.

24 As I evolve

It was in 2004 that I began the writing of this book and five years or so later, it is finally complete. At least I think it's complete. Who knows, after this is over, I might decide on a sequel!

I think the last time I looked at this manuscript was back in 2009. My thought was that one day..... I just might make it into an *e*-book and sell it to my real estate clients as a kind of guidebook.

I can tell you that no one was more surprised than I when a call came in from Manor Publishing House advising me that they would like to publish my book. Never in a million years did I think this would ever get published! (Well, apparently this manifesting stuff really works....as well as a little help from my friend!)

I had not laid eyes on this book in over two years and all of a sudden I had to go through the entire thing to make sure that what I said made sense to me if I wanted it to make sense to others. I also needed to ensure that I didn't repeat myself too many times. Well it did make sense and repetitions were removed in many different areas but there is a distinct possibility that I could have cut out more.... Oh well!

As I read through the pages it brings me back to where I used to be and then I realize how far I've come, how much I've evolved and how satisfied I am with my *self* and with my life. Back in the late '90's when I embarked on this new path, I had no idea where I would end up, mentally, physically or even spiritually. The latter being a foreign concept to me. My driving force was to find my inner happiness. A happiness that was not dictated by the things I owned or by the amount of money in my bank account or how many vacations I could afford.

To this day, I still reach out for help and when I do my Teachers suddenly appear to guide me along the way. Some of them are with me all of the time; also living more consciously makes me aware that they never too far. Learning is a never ending process and I know that I've missed some lessons along the way (my unconscious moments). I also know they will come to me in good time, when I least expect it and when I probably need it the most. I recognize that I am being constantly tested to see if I really have evolved. The people who used to be able to push my buttons matter no more because however hard they try, they can no longer find them.

Would I change anything? Hell no! The way I figure it, I woke up when I did because I was ready for change. There were times when it got to be too much, the challenges became struggles and my life felt like it was going nowhere fast. The great thing about these situations is that I quickly realized I could sit in my muck for as long as I liked or I could pick up a shovel and clear it all away.

The happiness that I have found along with my Spirituality have given me a deeper sense of peace and calm. I make my own choices and I actually learn from them. Some are good and some not so good but the point is that I am still learning. It's a great thing to know that I have a choice! I have Free Will!

May you discover your Truth, walk into your Power, embrace who you are and love yourself sincerely and deeply.

> Learning is implicit within an existence which is ever changing. Embrace it, find wisdom within it, and know that without it there would be no connection.
> ~ *Miykael*

About the Author

From the 1980's to 1995, Christine Mc Dowell was a Realtor on the West Island, Montreal, Quebec and ranked within the top 5%.

It was between 1997 and 2006 that Christine after much thought and consideration, chose to leave a very lucrative business, letting go of a five figure income, to search for true happiness.

With a Doctoral in Clinical Hypnosis and a Master Practitioner of NLP and Time Line Therapy™ Christine opened a private practice as a Life Skill/Style Coach. In her private practice, she helped hundreds of people identify and achieve their goals, overcome stress and begin the process of reconnecting with their true identity.

In 2006, Christine returned to Real Estate, reuniting with a people business she's long loved. As a result of the knowledge acquired as a Life Skill/Style Coach along with her training and education, she found that getting back into real estate was an easy transition. As Christine well knows, selling a home is very emotional. With her expertise on so many levels, her clients quickly find out that they've hired more than a Realtor.

Christine McDowell is a high energy life skills coach who brings a wealth of training and experience to her work as an expert in helping people make difficult transitions with ease.

Christine knows from first-hand experience how challenging life can be for people. She also knows how to turn those challenges into results that work wonders. This experience and expertise ultimately resulted in the writing/creation of her breakthrough book: **You're Not Broken – You Need to Harness Your Inner Power**

You're NOT Broken

Manor House Publishing Inc.
www.manor-house.biz
905-648-2193

www.ingramcontent.com/pod-product-compliance
Lightning Source LLC
Chambersburg PA
CBHW021111080526
44587CB00010B/482